CPM EXAM

FINANC ACCOUNTING AND REPORTING

FAR 2024

CPA EXAM REVIEW

Robert Smith

Copyright © 2024

No part of this publication may be reproduced, distributed, or transmitted in any form or by any means, including photocopying, recording, or other electronic or mechanical methods, without the prior written permission of the publisher, except in the case of brief quotations embodied in critical reviews and certain other noncommercial uses permitted by copy.

INDEX

INTRODUCTION TO ACCOUNTING 4
CHAPTER 1   FINANCIAL REPORTING NORMS SIMPLIFIED 5
CHAPTER 2 ADJUSTING ACCOUNTING CHANGES AND ERRORS 11
CHAPTER 3 INVENTORY MANAGEMENT 15
CHAPTER 4 CONSTRUCTION ACCOUNTING PRACTICES 20
CHAPTER 5 OPERATIONAL ASSET MANAGEMENT 23
CHAPTER 6 CURRENT MONETARY ASSETS AND LIABILITIES 27
CHAPTER 7 TIME VALUE, NOTES AND BONDS 37
CHAPTER 8 DEBT RESTRUCTURING TECHNIQUES 42
CHAPTER 9 LEASE ACCOUNTING 46
CHAPTER 10 TAXATION IN ACCOUNTING 50
CHAPTER 11 EQUITY AND STOCKHOLDERS' RIGHTS 54
CHAPTER 12 EARNINGS PER SHARE ANALYSIS 59
CHAPTER 13 INVESTMENT ACCOUNTING 62
CHAPTER 14 SIMULATED CASH METHOD 66
CHAPTER 15 CASH FLOW STATEMENT TECHNIQUES 69
CHAPTER 16 FINANCIAL STATEMENTS CONSOLIDATION 72
CHAPTER 17 CURRENCY EXCHANGE TRANSACTIONS 75
CHAPTER 18 PARTNERSHIP ACCOUNTING 78
CHAPTER 19 GOVERNMENTAL FUND ACCOUNTING 82
CHAPTER 20 NON- PROFIT FINANCIAL MANAGEMENT 87

INTRODUCTION TO ACCOUNTING

Accounting is an essential discipline that serves as the backbone of financial management across various sectors. It provides the systematic framework for recording, analyzing, and reporting financial information, enabling organizations to make informed decisions. This book aims to offer a comprehensive overview of key accounting concepts, focusing on financial management, monetary assets, liabilities, governmental accounting, and non-profit accounting.

Effective financial management is critical for both profitability and sustainability. It encompasses budgeting, forecasting, and strategic planning, ensuring that resources are allocated efficiently to achieve organizational goals. This book will guide readers through the principles of financial management, highlighting best practices and tools necessary for effective decision-making.

Monetary assets, including cash, investments, and receivables, are vital to an organization's operational health. Understanding how to manage and report these assets is crucial for maintaining liquidity and maximizing financial performance. This section will explore various types of monetary assets and the accounting standards that govern their valuation and reporting.

Liabilities represent obligations that organizations must meet in the future, impacting their financial stability. A thorough comprehension of both current and long-term liabilities is essential for sound financial planning and risk management. This book will delve into the classification of liabilities, their implications for financial statements, and strategies for effective management.

Governmental accounting presents unique challenges and requirements that differ from those in the private sector. It emphasizes accountability, transparency, and compliance in managing public funds. This book will cover the principles of governmental accounting, including fund accounting, budgetary controls, and the reporting standards that ensure fiscal responsibility.

Non-profit accounting focuses on the distinct financial practices of non-profit organizations, which operate under different motivations and regulations compared to for-profit entities. This section will address fund accounting, revenue recognition, and the preparation of financial statements that reflect the mission-driven nature of non-profits.

By integrating these critical topics, this book equips readers with a holistic understanding of accounting and financial management. Whether you are a student, a financial professional, or someone interested in enhancing your knowledge, this guide will provide the insights and tools necessary to navigate the complexities of accounting in various contexts.

CHAPTER 1
FINANCIAL REPORTING NORMS SIMPLIFIED

Financial reporting norms are the backbone of accurate and transparent financial communication. They guide companies on how to prepare and present their financial statements, ensuring consistency and reliability for investors, regulators, and other stakeholders.

This chapter provides a concise overview of the essential accounting principles, elements of financial statements, performance obligation, fair value measurements, and financial reporting requirements, including SEC reporting and balance sheet disclosures.

Elements of Financial Statements

Financial statements are composed of key elements that provide users with a complete picture of a company's financial performance and position. These elements include:

Element	Description	Example
Assets	Resources controlled by the entity as a result of past events, expected to bring future benefits.	Cash, inventory, property, and equipment.
Liabilities	Present obligations arising from past events, settlement of which is expected to result in an outflow of resources.	Loans, accounts payable, and accrued expenses.
Equity	Residual interest in the assets of the entity after deducting liabilities.	Common stock, retained earnings.
Income	Increases in economic benefits during the period in the form of inflows or enhancements of assets.	Sales revenue, interest income.
Expenses	Decreases in economic benefits during the period.	Cost of goods sold, salaries, and administrative expenses.

Example: A company with $500,000 in assets and $300,000 in liabilities has equity (or net assets) of $200,000, reflecting the owner's interest in the company.

Key Concepts in Financial Reporting

Concept	Description	Example
Materiality	Information is material if its omission could influence decisions made by users of financial reports.	A $10,000 error in a small business is material, but immaterial to a large corporation.
Historical Cost	Assets are recorded at their original purchase price.	Land purchased for $100,000 stays recorded at $100,000, even if its market value rises.
Fair Value	Assets and liabilities are measured at their current market value.	A stock purchased at $50, now worth $75, would be reported at $75 under fair value accounting.

Performance Obligation

In financial accounting, **performance obligations** are promises in a contract to transfer goods or services to a customer. Under the revenue recognition standard, a company recognizes revenue when it satisfies these performance obligations.

Step	Example
Identify the Obligation	A software company agrees to deliver and maintain a software license for one year. The performance obligations are delivering the software and providing ongoing maintenance.
Determine Timing	The software is delivered upfront, so the first performance obligation is satisfied at the point in time of delivery. The maintenance is provided over the year, so this obligation is satisfied over time.
Revenue Recognition	The company recognizes the revenue from the software upon delivery and recognizes the maintenance revenue over the year as services are performed.

This strategy guarantees that revenue is only recorded after the client has taken ownership of the items or services.

Fair Value Measurement

The phrase "fair value measurement" refers to the method by which the market participants on the measurement date might settle an obligation or sell an asset for the same price.

Fair Value Hierarchy

When measuring fair value, the Fair Value Hierarchy categorizes the inputs used to calculate the value into three levels:

Level	Inputs	Example
Level 1	Quoted prices in active markets for identical assets.	Stock prices from the New York Stock Exchange.
Level 2	Quoted prices for similar assets in inactive markets or observable inputs.	Real estate valued based on nearby property sales.
Level 3	Unobservable inputs based on assumptions.	Valuing a privately-held company's shares.

Example: A company's stock portfolio might include shares traded on a major stock exchange (Level 1), bonds for which prices are derived from market data (Level 2), and private equity investments that require estimations (Level 3).

Fair Value Option (FVO)

Financial assets and liabilities that qualify may be valued at fair market value if an entity chooses to do so via the Fair Value Option (FVO). The FVO is applied to the whole asset or obligation once chosen and cannot be reversed for that particular item.

Eligible Items	When to Apply FVO
Financial Assets	Loans, receivables, or investments in debt and equity securities.
Liabilities	Issued debt, guarantees, or obligations under derivatives.

Example: For its bond portfolio, a corporation selects the FVO. Thus, on each balance sheet date, the bonds are valued at fair market value, and any changes in value are shown in the income statement. The corporation might then adjust its asset values to reflect current market circumstances.

Revenue Recognition: Five-Step Model

Revenue is recognized when a company satisfies a performance obligation by transferring goods or services to the customer. The five-step model ensures that companies report revenue consistently and accurately:

1. Identify the contract with the customer.
2. Identify performance obligations within the contract.
3. Determine the transaction price.
4. Allocate the transaction price to performance obligations.
5. Recognize revenue when the performance obligation is satisfied.

Step	Example
Identify Contract	A company signs a contract to deliver 100 computers.
Identify Obligation	The obligation is to deliver the computers.
Determine Price	The contract price is $100,000.
Allocate Price	Allocate $1,000 per computer.
Recognize Revenue	Revenue is recognized as each computer is delivered.

Comparative Financial Statements

Financial data for at least two reporting periods must be shown in comparative financial statements, which are a requirement for publicly traded corporations. A better view of the financial health of a business over time is produced by this.

Filing Status	10-K (Annual Report)	10-Q (Quarterly Report)
Non-accelerated filer	90 days after year-end	45 days after quarter-end
Accelerated filer	75 days after year-end	40 days after quarter-end
Large Accelerated filer	60 days after year-end	40 days after quarter-end

Example: A large accelerated filer, such as a Fortune 500 company, must file its annual report within 60 days after the fiscal year ends. This ensures timely reporting to stakeholders..

Comprehensive Income: Beyond Net Income

Any change in equity that is not attributable to owner-to-owner transactions is accounted for in comprehensive income. By adding up all of a company's earnings and losses, not just net income, it paints a fuller picture of how well the business is doing financially.

Net Income	Other Comprehensive Income (OCI)
Revenue from operations, minus expenses.	Unrealized gains/losses on available-for-sale securities, foreign currency translation adjustments.

Example: The primary business activities of a corporation result in a net income of $5 million. Complementing its $6 million in comprehensive income are the $1 million in unrealized profits from overseas assets that are recognized in OCI.

SEC Reporting Requirements

Public companies in the United States must comply with reporting requirements set by the **Securities and Exchange Commission (SEC).** These requirements include filing annual and quarterly reports, which are essential for providing transparency to investors.

Filing Status	10-K (Annual Report)	10-Q (Quarterly Report)
Non-accelerated filer	90 days after year-end	45 days after quarter-end
Accelerated filer	75 days after year-end	40 days after quarter-end
Large Accelerated filer	60 days after year-end	40 days after quarter-end

Example: A big technology company or other significant expedited filer is required to submit its audited financial statements, management discussion and analysis, and annual 10-K report no later than 60 days after the end of the fiscal year.

Disclosures of Balance Sheet Date

A disclosure is considered subsequent if it is made after the balance sheet date and occurs after the reporting period but before the financial statements are released. There are two main categories for these occurrences:

Type of Event	Action Required	Example
Adjusting Event	Affects conditions existing at the balance sheet date and requires adjustment of the financial statements.	A company settles a lawsuit after year-end, related to events that occurred before the year-end.
Non-Adjusting Event	Relates to conditions that arose after the balance sheet date and requires disclosure in the notes but not adjustment of the financials.	A major customer goes bankrupt after year-end, but the event didn't exist at the balance sheet date..

Example: While the financial statements would not be adjusted, the notes would be updated to reflect the fact that an important customer filed for bankruptcy soon after the balance sheet date, even though the client had no prior financial issues.

Substantial Doubt About Going Concern

A corporation is required to declare in its financial statements any serious uncertainty over its capacity to continue operations, often known as going concern. Considerations include problems with money, operational losses, or substantial debt.

Condition	Action
Probable inability to meet obligations.	Disclose in the notes to financial statements.
Efforts to mitigate doubt.	Include plans to address liquidity concerns.

Example: For example, a retail shop that is seeing a decline in sales and an increase in indebtedness might reveal in its financial statement that it is seriously considering ceasing operations. It adds that it intends to reduce expenses and reorganize debt.

Conclusion

Rules established by the SEC, generally accepted accounting principles (GAAP), international financial reporting standards (IFRS), and others provide the backbone of reliable financial reporting. A complete picture of a business's financial health may be presented with the use of financial statements, performance commitments, fair value measures, and the Fair Value Option. Transparency and confidence in the markets are maintained by compliance with SEC reporting requirements and disclosures of subsequent events.

The rest of these chapters will delve into these topics through illustrative examples from the real world and their implications for business decisions in the current, interwoven global economy.

CHAPTER 2
ADJUSTING ACCOUNTING CHANGES AND ERRORS

Nobody gets to be perfect in the world of accounting. The adjustments are whether it's a change in accounting principles, an error in reporting, these adjustments are important to maintaining the accuracy and integrity of financial statements. In this chapter, we'll explain the different kinds of accounting changes, how to take care of errors and the different ways to get financial reports correct.

Types of Accounting Changes

Accounting changes fall into three broad categories: changes in accounting principle, changes in accounting estimate, and changes in reporting entities. Each type of change requires a distinct approach to adjustment.

Type of Change	Description	Example
Change in Principle	An accounting policy that converts one generally accepted accounting principle to another.	Switching from the completed-contract method to the percentage-of-completion method in construction accounting.
Change in Estimate	Adjustments due to new information or experiences that alter assumptions.	Revising the useful life of a depreciable asset from 10 years to 8 years based on new maintenance data.
Change in Reporting Entity	Happens when a business decides to alter the entities included in consolidation.	A merger that leads to the consolidation of a new subsidiary into the parent company's financial statements.

Approach for Adjustments:

- **Retrospective Approach:** Assuming the new accounting principle has been in use continuously, this procedure entails making adjustments to the financial statements of previous periods. When accounting rules are changed or mistakes in earlier periods are corrected, this method is used.

- **Prospective Approach:** This approach applies changes moving forward and is typically used for changes in accounting estimates, such as depreciation or amortization.

Adjusting for Errors

Errors in financial statements can arise from a variety of sources, such as mathematical mistakes, incorrect application of accounting principles, or oversight of information. When errors are identified, they must be corrected to maintain accurate financial reporting.

Errors typically affect multiple financial periods, and adjustments may be required for both the current and previous periods.

Example of Inventory Misstatement:

Consider a company that discovers it had understated ending inventory by $10,000 in 20XX. Given a tax rate of 30%, the necessary journal entry to correct this error would be:

Date	Account	Debit	Credit
11/3/20XX	Retained Earnings	$7,000	
	Inventory	$3,000	
	Taxes Payable		$10,000

This journal entry corrects the error by adjusting the inventory balance and taxes payable while impacting retained earnings. Such adjustments ensure that future financial statements accurately reflect the company's performance..

Impact of Misstated Inventory on Financial Statements:

Period	Inventory Adjustment	Net Income	Retained Earnings
"Beginning Inventory	True Balance	+$10,000	
Ending Inventory	True Balance	+$10,000	
Cost of Goods Sold"	Overstated by $10,000	Decreased	
Retained Earnings	Understated by $7,000		Corrected via entry

Adjusting for Changes in Accounting Principles

When a company changes its accounting principles, it must apply the retrospective approach to ensure comparability across financial periods. This involves revisiting past financial statements and making adjustments as if the new principle had always been in place.

Old Principle	New Principle	Action Required
FIFO	LIFO	Revise prior period financial statements to reflect the new inventory valuation method.
Percentage of Completion	Completed Contract	Adjust all affected prior periods for a consistent application of the new method.

Example: A construction company's revenue recognition and balance sheet will be affected when it moves from the percentage-of-completion approach to the completed-contract method, and it will be necessary to amend preceding periods to reflect this shift.

Fair Value Adjustments and Accounting Errors

Fair value measurement plays a critical role in many accounting adjustments, especially in financial instruments, asset revaluations, and impairment assessments.

Adjustment Type	Description	Example
Fair Value Change	Re-measurement of assets/liabilities to reflect current market conditions.	An investment in securities revalued due to market volatility.
Error in Fair Value Estimate	Recalculate the fair value of assets or liabilities for prior periods.	Incorrect application of a fair value model for a derivative contract.

Errors in fair value measurement require correction to accurately reflect the true financial position of the company. This is often done using the retrospective approach to ensure that past financial statements are corrected.

SEC Reporting: Adjusting Changes and Errors

Public companies are required to disclose the impact of accounting changes and errors in their financial reports, as per the SEC's requirements. This includes providing a description of the change, the rationale behind it, and the financial effects.

Required Disclosure	Content	Example
Nature of Change	Description of the accounting principle or estimate that changed.	The company changed its method of inventory valuation from FIFO to LIFO...
Rationale	Explanation of why the change was necessary.	This change better aligns the company's inventory costing with industry practices...
Financial Impact	Quantification of the effects on income, assets, liabilities, and equity.	The change resulted in a decrease in net income by $500,000 for the year...

Disclosures After Balance Sheet Date

Any events that happen after the balance sheet date but before the financial statements are produced are required to be disclosed by the company. The financial statements may need to be adjusted or a remark may suffice to describe these occurrences.

Event Type	Action Required	Example
Adjusting Event	Adjust financial statements if the event provides additional evidence of conditions that existed at the balance sheet date.	Lawsuit settlement related to pre-balance sheet date events.
Non-Adjusting Event	Disclose in notes if the event is significant but did not affect the balance sheet date conditions.	Acquisition of a new subsidiary after the balance sheet date.

Example: If a company settles a significant lawsuit after the balance sheet date but the underlying event occurred before the date, the financial statements must be adjusted to reflect this.

Conclusion

The integrity of financial reporting is maintained by adjusting for accounting changes and mistakes. In order to rectify mistakes, update accounting standards, or determine fair value, these adjustments are necessary for a genuine and accurate portrayal of a business's financial situation. Companies maintain their reliability and transparency by reporting according to recognized processes, such as retrospective and prospective. In order to explore how to put accounting changes and mistakes into effect, this chapter provides helpful background information. The next chapter will start to delve into more complex areas of financial accounting.

CHAPTER 3
INVENTORY MANAGEMENT

Inventory is certainly one of the most important balance sheet items for any company. Inventory is a major investment for firms manufacturing, retailing, or distributing and the management of inventory can affect profitability and cash flow and the efficiency of operations significantly. The remainder of the chapter will focus on key inventory management concepts, the systems used to track inventory, and methods to measure the value of inventory, as well as their strategic implications.

Understanding Inventory

Goods held for sale in the ordinary course of business, or goods that are in the process of being manufactured for sale, are included in inventory. According to this, companies would sell or use it within one year or their operating cycle, whichever is more. Hence it is classified as a current asset.

Types of Inventory:

- **Raw Materials**: Inputs used in the production process.
- **Work-in-Process:** Partially completed products still in the production process.
- **Finished Goods:** Completed products ready for sale.

Shipping Terms and Inventory Recognition:

- **FOB Shipping Point:** Ownership of the inventory transfers to the buyer when goods leave the seller's premises. The buyer records the inventory during transit.
- **FOB Destination:** Ownership transfers to the buyer when goods arrive at the buyer's location. The buyer records the inventory only upon receipt.

Example: If a retailer buys 1,000 units of product FOB Shipping Point, they would record the inventory on their balance sheet as soon as it leaves the supplier's warehouse, even though they haven't received it yet.

Inventory Tracking Systems

Inventory tracking systems help companies monitor and manage their inventory levels. The two main systems are the **Perpetual System** and the **Periodic System.**

System	Description	Example
Perpetual System	Continuously updates inventory records after each transaction. Every sale and purchase is immediately recorded in the system, making the perpetual system more accurate for real-time inventory tracking.	A supermarket uses barcode scanning at checkout, which automatically adjusts its inventory records as items are sold.
Periodic System	Updates inventory records at the end of the accounting period. Companies count their inventory physically, and cost of goods sold (COGS) is calculated at the end of the period. This system is less accurate than the perpetual system for real-time tracking but may be sufficient for smaller businesses.	A local bookstore performs an inventory count quarterly to update its financial records.

Example of Perpetual System Journal Entry: When a company purchases inventory:

Inventory	$	1,000
cr. Accounts payable	$	1,000

Example of Periodic System Journal Entry: When a company purchases inventory:

dr. Purchases	$	1,000
cr. Accounts	$	1,000

At the end of the period, COGS is calculated as:

COGS = Beginning Inventory + Net Purchases - Ending Inventory

Inventory Valuation Methods

Valuing inventory correctly is crucial for accurate financial reporting. The method chosen can significantly impact reported earnings, taxes, and decision-making. Below are the most commonly used methods for inventory valuation:

1. **First-In, First-Out (FIFO):**

- Assumes that the first items purchased (first-in) are the first items sold (first-out). The remaining inventory is valued at the most recent purchase prices.

- **Strategic Implication**: In periods of rising prices, FIFO results in lower COGS and higher net income because older, cheaper inventory is recorded as sold first.

- **Example:** If a company has 300 units at $1.30, 200 units at $1.40, and sells 350 units, FIFO assumes the oldest 300 units were sold first, followed by 50 units from the next layer.

2. **Last-In, First-Out (LIFO):**

- Assumes that the most recent items purchased (last-in) are the first items sold (first-out). The remaining inventory is valued at older prices.

- **Strategic Implication:** In periods of rising prices, LIFO results in higher COGS and lower net income because newer, more expensive inventory is sold first. This method can lead to tax savings in inflationary environments.

- **Example:** If the same company sells 350 units, LIFO assumes that the newest 200 units are sold first, followed by 150 units from the previous layer.

3. **Weighted Average:**

- This method calculates a weighted average cost per unit of inventory and applies this average to determine COGS and ending inventory.

- **Strategic Implication:** Weighted Average smooths out price fluctuations and provides a moderate financial impact compared to FIFO and LIFO.

- **Example:** If a company has 300 units at $1.30 and 200 units at $1.40, the weighted average cost per unit would be $1.34.

Cost Basis for Pricing Inventory (Example):

Date	Units	Unit Cost	Total Cost
1/1	300	$1.30	$390
1/10	200	$1.40	$280
1/25	100	$1.60	$160

Under FIFO (Perpetual System):

- The first 300 units are sold at $1.30 each.
- The next 50 units are sold at $1.40 each.
- **COGS = $460**

Under LIFO (Perpetual System):

- The last 200 units are sold at $1.40 each.
- The next 150 units are sold at $1.30 each.
- **COGS = $475**

Inventory Impairment and Write-Downs

Inventory is initially recorded at cost. However, if the market value of inventory falls below its cost, accounting standards require companies to write down the value of their inventory. The two main methods used for impairment are:

1. **Lower of Cost or Net Realizable Value (LCNRV):**

- Applied to FIFO and Average Cost methods. Inventory is written down to the lower of its cost or its net realizable value (NRV), which is the estimated selling price minus costs to complete and sell the inventory.

2. **Lower of Cost or Market (LCM):**

- Applied to LIFO. Inventory is written down to the lower of its cost or market value, where the market value cannot be higher than NRV or lower than NRV minus normal profit margins (floor).

Example:

dr. Cost of Goods Sold	$ 500,00
cr. Inventory	$ 500,00

Special Inventory Situations: Consignments

Consignment occurs when a company (the consignor) transfers goods to another party (the consignee) to sell on its behalf, but retains ownership of the goods until they are sold.

Consignor	Consignee (Sales Agent)
RETAINS ownership of the inventory. The inventory remains on the consignor's balance sheet until sold.	Receives a commission for selling the inventory and records the commission as revenue.
Records sales commission as an expense.	Does not record the inventory as an asset.

Example: If a company consigns $10,000 of inventory to a sales agent and the agent sells $6,000 worth, the company records:

dr. Accounts Receivable	$ 6,000
cr. Revenue	$ 6,000
dr. Cost of Goods Sold	$ 4,000
cr. Inventory	$ 4,000

The consignee records the sales commission earned, but does not include the inventory on its balance sheet.

Conclusion

Inventory management is an important process that involves financial performance, efficiency and decision making. Using the right inventory tracking system and valuation method, companies can better portray their financial condition and make the best inventory planning decisions. At the end of this chapter, we laid out the foundational concepts of inventory management and gave you the tools to really understand and apply these principles. In the next chapter, we will explore the complexities of revenue recognition and its significant role in financial reporting.

CHAPTER 4
CONSTRUCTION ACCOUNTING PRACTICES

With projects lasting for an extended period, construction accounting brings its own unique challenges, requiring a means to accurately report costs, revenues, and profits over time. This chapter will focus on two widely used **methods in construction accounting**: the Percentage of Completion Method and the Completed Contract Method. Both recognize revenue and profits in a different way depending on the stage of the project's life cycle.

Percentage of Completion Method

The **Percentage of Completion Method** is commonly used when cost estimates are reliable and the project spans multiple accounting periods. This method allows the contractor to recognize revenue and gross profit as the project progresses, based on the percentage of costs incurred relative to the total estimated costs.

Formula: Cumulative Revenue = (Cumulative Cost ÷ Estimated Total Cost) × Contract Price

This method aligns revenue recognition with the work completed, providing a more accurate picture of the contractor's financial performance over time.

Example:

Consider a construction contract with a total price of $1,000. By the end of 20X1, $200 in costs have been incurred, with a future estimated cost of $900. The journal entry to recognize this revenue is:

Year	Cost Incurred	Estimated Future Cost	Cumulative Revenue	Journal Entries
20X1	$200	$900	$222	dr. Construction in Progress $200
				dr. Expense $200
				cr. Revenue $222

As more costs are incurred in the following years, the revenue recognized adjusts accordingly.

Strategic Implication: The **Percentage of Completion Method** allows a company to report steady earnings as long as the project progresses as expected. This method works best for contractors who need to provide accurate interim financial reports and who have high confidence in their cost estimates.

Completed Contract Method

The **Completed Contract** Method is used when it is difficult to estimate total costs or when the duration of the project is short. Under this method, no revenue or profit is recognized until the project is complete.

All costs are accumulated in the **Construction in Progress** account, and revenue is only recognized when the project reaches completion.

Example: A contractor working on a $1,000 project in 20X1 incurs $200 in costs. The project is completed in 20X3. The journal entries throughout the period would be recorded, but no revenue is recognized until completion.

Year	Journal Entries
20X1	dr. Construction in Progress $200
	cr. Accounts Payable $200
20X3	dr. Billings $1,000
	cr. Revenue $1,000

Strategic Implication: To be more frugal, the Completed Contract Method waits to record revenue until the project is fully completed. Industries whose expenses are very unpredictable or where project durations are quite short might benefit from this approach.

Comparing the Methods

Aspect	Percentage of Completion	Completed Contract
Revenue Recognition	Revenue is recognized as work progresses, based on the percentage completed.	Revenue is recognized only when the project is fully completed.
Profit Recognition	Profits are recognized progressively over time.	Profits are recognized only at the end of the project.
Suitability	Best for long-term contracts with reliable cost estimates.	Best for short-term projects or projects with uncertain costs.

Real-World Application: Companies that undertake long-term infrastructure projects, such as highways or bridges, often use the **Percentage of Completion Method** to match costs with revenues over the life of the project. On the other hand, smaller contractors who handle short-term renovations might prefer the **Completed Contract** Method to simplify their accounting.

Journal Entries for Construction Accounting

In construction accounting, proper journal entries ensure that all costs and revenues are correctly allocated throughout the project. Below are examples of journal entries for both methods:

Percentage of Completion Method (20X2):

dr. Construction in Progress	$	300
dr. Expense	$	300
cr. Revenue	$	327
dr. Cash	$	320
Cr. Billings	$	320

Completed Contract Method (20X3):

dr. Construction in Progress	$	930
dr. Expense	$	930
cr. Revenue	$	1,000
dr. Cash	$	1,000
Cr. Billings	$	1,000

These entries reflect how costs and revenues are recorded as work progresses or when a project is fully completed.

Conclusion

For such extended project timelines, construction accounting requires specialized practices to enable appropriate financial reporting. The Percentage of Completion Method is appropriate when there are reliable cost estimates and revenue and profits can be recognized in progress. Finally, the Completed Contract Method has a more conservative way of recognizing revenue and profit, doing so only when the contract is finished. But understanding which method to apply and how to record these transactions is key to being able to properly reflect a contractor's financial health. The next chapter will focus on some advanced cost management techniques to achieve profitability on construction projects.

CHAPTER 5
OPERATIONAL ASSET MANAGEMENT

Any organization that produces goods or services relies on its operational assets. Both tangible and intangible assets are these long term investments used by companies to generate revenue for multiple years. In this chapter, we will examine different categories of operational assets, the approach to managing and depreciating them, and how strategic considerations shape decisions about asset management.

Understanding Operational Assets

Operational assets are non-current assets that companies use in their day-to-day operations. They are categorized into two broad types:

Category	Description	Examples
Fixed Assets (Property, Plant, and Equipment)	Tangible, non-current assets used in production.	Land, buildings, machinery, vehicles, and equipment.
Intangible Assets	Non-physical, non-current assets that provide future benefits.	Patents, trademarks, goodwill, software, and copyrights.

And both types of assets are vital to keeping a business producing and continuing to prosper. These assets can be managed properly, giving rise to increased efficiency, reduced costs and increase in profitability.

Capitalizing Costs for Fixed Assets

The cost of fixed assets is recorded on the balance sheet with all the expenses that are required to purchase an asset and ready it to use. We call this process capitalization.

Asset	Capitalized Costs
Land	Purchase price, legal fees, title fees, clearing, grading, and demolition of existing structures.
Buildings and Equipment	Purchase price, construction costs, freight, installation, and interest during construction.

Example: Company bought $10,000 in a piece of machinery. Besides the purchase price, it charges $500 in freight charges and $1,000 for installation. These costs are capitalized and $11,500 is recorded on the balance sheet as the total asset value.

Depreciation of Fixed Assets

Allocating the cost of a fixed asset over its useful life is called depreciation. Essentially, we want the asset to cost the same as the revenue it's capable of producing. There are several methods for calculating depreciation:

1. **Straight-Line Depreciation:** This method spreads the asset's cost evenly over its useful life.
2. **Double Declining Balance:** This accelerated method applies a higher depreciation rate in the early years of the asset's life.
3. **Units of Production:** Depreciation on an asset is based on how the asset is used, either on the number of units produced or on the number of hours utilized.

Example of Depreciation for an Asset Purchased at $1,000 (5-Year Life, $100 Salvage Value):

Year	Straight Line	Double Declining	Units of Production (Based on Output)
20X1	$180	$400	$225 (Based on 250 units)
20X2	$180	$240	$270 (Based on 300 units)

Strategic Implication: The depreciation effects on the income statement and balance sheet. Take, for example, choosing an accelerated depreciation method such as Double Declining Balance may lower taxable income in the early years of an asset's life, while the Straight Line Depreciation method has a consistent expense over time, making it easier to forecast long term profitability.

Managing Intangible Assets

Although intangible assets have no physical form, many of them are often critical to a company's competitive advantage. Patents, which protect technology innovation, and trademarks, which secure brand identity are just two examples of exclusive rights for which they have considerable value.

Capitalizing Intangibles:

- **Purchased Intangibles:** The purchase price, legal fees, and registration fees are capitalized.
- **Internally Developed Intangibles:** Most costs are expensed as incurred, except for certain qualifying costs like legal fees related to patent filing or software development costs.

Example: A company develops a new software platform internally. Costs related to research and development are expensed immediately, while legal fees to secure a software patent are capitalized.

Exchange of Operational Assets

When companies exchange assets, the treatment of gains and losses depends on whether the exchange has **commercial substance** meaning it changes the future cash flows of the company.

Setting	Gain Recognition
Exchange Without Commercial Substance	No gain is recognized if cash is not involved. If cash (boot) is involved, partial gains are recognized.
Exchange With Commercial Substance	Full gain or loss is recognized.

Example: A company exchanges an old machine (book value $1,000) for a new machine worth $1,500. If the exchange lacks commercial substance and no cash is involved, the company does not recognize any gain. However, if the company receives $500 in cash as part of the exchange, a portion of the gain will be recognized.

Impairment of Operational Assets

Operational assets are tested for impairment when there is evidence that their carrying value may not be recoverable. The impairment test involves comparing the asset's carrying value (CV) to its recoverable amount, either fair value (FV) or net realizable value (NRV).

Asset Type	Test for Loss	Calculation of Loss	Depreciation After Impairment?
Tangible Assets	CV > Non-Discounted Cash Flows	CV - Fair Value	Yes
Intangible Assets (Finite Life)	CV > Non-Discounted Cash Flows	CV - Fair Value	Yes
Intangible Assets (Indefinite Life)	CV > Fair Value	CV - Fair Value	No
Goodwill	CV of Reporting Unit > FV of Reporting Unit	CV Reporting Unit - FV Reporting Unit	No

Example: An office building for impairment is assessed by a company. If the economic benefit of the building is less than its carrying value, the building is written down to its fair value, at which time an impairment loss is recognized on the carrying value of the building.

Conclusion

Operational asset management is essential to the long term success of a company. Companies can optimize the use of their assets using the right costs, with the right depreciation methods, and through effective management of intangible assets and exchanges, to enhance the financial performance.

This allows you to assess how the balances of the depreciation and impairment relate to the current value of the company's operational assets. In the next chapter, we will examine the acceleration of profitability and long term growth possible through operational and strategic cost management.

CHAPTER 6
CURRENT MONETARY ASSETS AND LIABILITIES

But a company's liquidity and financial health depend on its current monetary assets and liabilities. Poor management of these assets and liabilities can have a huge impact on cash flow, profitability and the ability to meet short term obligations. The focus is on monetary assets and liabilities of current types like cash and accounts receivable, payroll liabilities, and warranties, and attempts practical accounting treatments and strategic considerations.

Monetary Assets and Liabilities Defined

Type	Description
Monetary Asset	Assets that can be converted to a fixed amount of cash without reference to future prices.
Monetary Liability	Obligations to pay fixed amounts of cash or fulfill specific obligations.
Non-Monetary Asset/Liability	Items whose value depends on future prices or production. Examples include inventory (asset) and deferred income (liability).

Examples of Monetary Assets:

- **Cash and Cash Equivalents:** Cash on hand, certificates of deposit, money market funds, and Treasury bills with original maturities of 3 months or less.
- **Accounts Receivable:** Claims to receive cash for goods sold or services rendered.

Cash Equivalents and Restricted Cash

Cash Equivalents are short-term, highly liquid investments with original maturities of three months or less. Examples include Treasury bills, money market funds, and commercial paper. Cash equivalents are often included with cash on the balance sheet because they are so readily convertible into cash.

Restricted Cash is cash that is set aside for a specific purpose, such as debt repayment, capital expenditures, or as part of a compensating balance agreement with a bank. Restricted cash must be disclosed separately in the financial statements to reflect its unavailability for general use.

Example: A company with a compensating balance of $2,000 held as a condition of a loan would separate that amount from its general cash balance.

Accounts Receivable and Bad Debt

Accounts receivable represent claims for payment from customers for goods delivered or services provided. However, not all receivables will be collected, which is where the **Allowance for Uncollectible Accounts** comes in.

The **Allowance** Method is the GAAP-compliant way to account for bad debt. It involves estimating uncollectible accounts and creating an allowance to reflect potential losses.

Journal Entries	Explanation
dr. Accounts Receivable $2,000	Initial recording of revenue and the corresponding receivable.
cr. Revenue $2,000	
dr. Bad Debt Expense $150	Estimate of uncollectible accounts.
cr. Allowance for Uncollectible Accounts $150	Creation of the allowance.
dr. Allowance for Uncollectible Accounts $50	Writing off a specific uncollectible account.
cr. Accounts Receivable $50	

Strategic Insight: Managing accounts receivable effectively can improve cash flow and reduce the need for external financing. Estimating bad debt accurately helps maintain a realistic view of the company's net receivables, protecting against overstatement of assets.

Financing with Receivables

When companies need to improve liquidity, they can use their receivables to raise cash through **Factoring or Assignment of Receivables.**

1. **Factoring:** The company sells its receivables to a financial institution at a discount in exchange for immediate cash.

   - **With Recourse:** The company retains some risk if the receivables aren't collected.

   - **Without Recourse:** The financial institution assumes the risk, and the company has no further obligation.

2. **Assignment:** The company borrows money, using receivables as collateral. If the loan defaults, the financial institution has a claim on the receivables.

Example: A company factors $100,000 of receivables with recourse for $90,000. The factoring fee is 2%, and the company retains liability for any uncollected amounts.

dr. Cash	$ 90,000
dr. Loss on Sale Receivables	$ 2,000
dr. Receivable from Factor	$ 8,000
dr. Accounts Receivable	$ 100,000

Payroll Liabilities

Payroll liabilities include employee compensation and the employer's obligations for taxes and benefits. These liabilities must be recognized as they accrue.

Components of Payroll Liabilities

Federal and State Taxes: Income tax withholding and employer payroll taxes (FICA, unemployment taxes).

Employee Benefits: Health insurance, 401(k) contributions, and other benefits.

Example: A company incurs payroll expenses, including salary and employer-matched 401(k) contributions.

dr. Salary Expence	$ 10,000
dr. 401(k) Employer Expence	$ 500
cr. Cash	$ 9,500 (Net Pay)
dr. Payroll Tax Liability	$ 500
cr. Employer 401(k) Payable	$ 500

Strategic Insight: Proper management of payroll liabilities is essential for cash flow planning. Offering employee benefits like health insurance or retirement contributions can also impact payroll costs but may improve employee retention and productivity.

Contingent Liabilities and Warranties

Contingent Liabilities arise from potential obligations that depend on the outcome of future events, such as lawsuits or product warranties.

Likelihood of Event	Action
Probable	Recognize the liability and disclose.
Reasonably Possible	Disclose only.
Remote	No action required.

Example: A company estimates that its warranty claims will cost $750 during the current year. It recognizes the warranty liability when it makes the sale.

dr. Warranty Expence	$	750
dr. Warranty Liability	$	750

If the event is **reasonably** possible but not probable, the company would simply disclose the potential liability without recording it on the balance sheet.

Ratios and Turnover Metrics

Proper management of current assets and liabilities directly impacts key financial ratios that measure liquidity and efficiency.

Ratio	Formula
Current Ratio	Current Assets ÷ Current Liabilities
Quick Ratio	(Cash + Receivables + Short-Term Investments) ÷ Current Liabilities

Turnover Metrics: Turnover measures how efficiently a company manages its assets.

Metric	Formula
Accounts Receivable Turnover	Net Sales ÷ Average Accounts Receivable
Inventory Turnover	Cost of Goods Sold ÷ Average Inventory

Example: A company has $1,000,000 in net sales and $200,000 in average accounts receivable. Its accounts receivable turnover ratio is 5, meaning the company collects its receivables five times per year.

Strategic Insight: Higher turnover ratios indicate efficient asset management, while lower ratios may signal inefficiencies or potential liquidity issues.

Monetary Assets and Liabilities Defined

Type	Description
Monetary Asset	Assets that can be converted to a fixed amount of cash without reference to future prices.
Monetary Liability	Obligations to pay fixed amounts of cash or fulfill specific obligations.
Non-Monetary Asset/Liability	Items whose value depends on future prices or production. Examples include inventory (asset) and deferred income (liability).

Examples of Monetary Assets:

- **Cash and Cash Equivalents:** Cash on hand, certificates of deposit, money market funds, and Treasury bills with original maturities of 3 months or less.
- **Accounts Receivable:** Claims to receive cash for goods sold or services rendered.

Cash Equivalents and Restricted Cash

Cash Equivalents are short-term, highly liquid investments with original maturities of three months or less. Examples include Treasury bills, money market funds, and commercial paper. Cash equivalents are included with cash on the balance sheet because they are so readily convertible into cash.

Restricted Cash is cash set aside for specific purposes, such as debt repayment, capital expenditures, or as part of a compensating balance agreement with a bank. Restricted cash is disclosed separately in the financial statements to reflect its unavailability for general use.

Example: A company with a compensating balance of $2,000 held as a condition of a loan would separate that amount from its general cash balance.

Accruals: A Key Element of Liabilities

Accruals are expenses that have been incurred but not yet paid or revenues that have been earned but not yet received. They represent obligations or receivables that need to be recognized in the financial statements during the period in which they are incurred, even though the cash transaction occurs later.

Examples of Accrued Liabilities:

- **Salaries Payable:** Employee wages earned but not yet paid by the end of the period.
- **Interest Payable:** Interest on loans that has accrued but not yet been paid.
- **Taxes Payable:** Taxes that are owed but not yet paid.

Example: A company accrues $500 for employee salaries at the end of the year, recognizing the liability in the period it is incurred.

| dr. Salary Expense | $ | 500 |
| cr. Salaries Payable | $ | 500 |

Strategic Insight: Accrual accounting provides a more accurate picture of a company's financial position by matching revenues and expenses to the period in which they occur, regardless of when cash is exchanged. This is essential for assessing the company's true profitability and for making informed business decisions.

Vacation Accruals

Vacation accruals represent a company's obligation to pay employees for vacation time that has been earned but not yet taken. Under accrual accounting, these liabilities are recognized as employees earn their vacation time, even if they do not take it until a later period.

Example: A company's employees earn 5,000 hours of vacation time during the year, but 2,000 hours are unused at year-end. The company accrues for the cost of the unused vacation time to reflect its obligation.

| dr. Salary Expence | $ | 500 |
| Cr. Vacation Accrual Liability | $ | 500 |

If the employee takes the vacation in the following year, the liability is reduced as the vacation is used:

| dr. Vacation Accrual Liability | $ | 500 |
| Cr. Cash | $ | 500 |

Strategic Insight: Proper accounting for vacation accruals ensures that companies accurately reflect their future obligations on the balance sheet. It also helps in budgeting and forecasting future payroll expenses, particularly for large organizations with significant employee benefits.

Accounts Receivable and Bad Debt

Accounts receivable represent claims for payment from customers for goods delivered or services provided. However, not all receivables will be collected, which is where the **Allowance for Uncollectible Accounts** comes in.

The **Allowance** Method is the GAAP-compliant way to account for bad debt. It involves estimating uncollectible accounts and creating an allowance to reflect potential losses.

Journal Entries	Explanation
dr. Accounts Receivable $2,000	Initial recording of revenue and the corresponding receivable.
cr. Revenue $2,000	
dr. Bad Debt Expense $150	Estimate of uncollectible accounts.
cr. Allowance for Uncollectible Accounts $150	Creation of the allowance.
dr. Allowance for Uncollectible Accounts $50	Writing off a specific uncollectible account.
cr. Accounts Receivable $50	

Strategic Insight: Managing accounts receivable effectively can improve cash flow and reduce the need for external financing. Estimating bad debt accurately helps maintain a realistic view of the company's net receivables, protecting against overstatement of assets.

Financing with Receivables

When companies need to improve liquidity, they can use their receivables to raise cash through **Factoring or Assignment of Receivables.**

1. **Factoring:** The company sells its receivables to a financial institution at a discount in exchange for immediate cash.

   - **With Recourse:** The company retains some risk if the receivables aren't collected.
   - **Without Recourse:** The financial institution assumes the risk, and the company has no further obligation.

2. **Assignment:** The company borrows money, using receivables as collateral. If the loan defaults, the financial institution has a claim on the receivables.

Example: A company factors $100,000 of receivables with recourse for $90,000. The factoring fee is 2%, and the company retains liability for any uncollected amounts.

dr. Cash	$ 90,000
dr. Loss on Sale of Receivables	$ 2,000
dr. Receivable from Factor	$ 8,000
cr. Accounts Receivable	$ 100,000

Payroll Liabilities

Payroll liabilities include employee compensation and the employer's obligations for taxes and benefits. These liabilities must be recognized as they accrue.

CPM EXAM

> **Components of Payroll Liabilities**
>
> **Federal and State Taxes:** Income tax withholding and employer payroll taxes (FICA, unemployment taxes).
>
> **Employee Benefits:** Health insurance, 401(k) contributions, and other benefits.

Example: A company incurs payroll expenses, including salary and employer-matched 401(k) contributions.

dr. Salary Expence	$ 10,000
dr. 401(k) Employer Expence	$ 500
cr. Cash	$ 9,500 (Net Pay)
cr. Payroll Tax Liability	$ 500
dr. Employer 401(k) Payable	$ 500

Strategic Insight: Proper management of payroll liabilities is essential for cash flow planning. Offering employee benefits like health insurance or retirement contributions can also impact payroll costs but may improve employee retention and productivity."

Warranties

Warranties are a form of contingent liability that companies must account for based on the expected cost of fulfilling warranty claims. There are two types of warranties: **Assurance-Type Warranties and Service-Type Warranties.**

- **Assurance-Type Warranties:** These warranties ensure that the product will function as intended. The liability for these warranties is recognized at the time of sale.

- **Service-Type Warranties:** These warranties are sold separately from the product, and the revenue related to them is recognized over the period the warranty covers.

Example: A company sells a product with a $5,000 assurance-type warranty. The estimated cost of warranty claims is $1,250, and the company recognizes the liability and expense upon sale.

dr. Warranty Expence	$ 1,250
cr. Warranty Liability	$ 1,250

As warranty claims are made, the liability is reduced:

dr. Warranty Liability	$ 750
dr. Cash	$ 750

Strategic Insight: Warranty liabilities must be carefully estimated to avoid understating expenses. Proper accounting for warranties helps companies manage future obligations and ensure their financial statements accurately reflect potential costs.

Contingent Liabilities

Contingent Liabilities arise from potential obligations that depend on the outcome of future events, such as lawsuits or product warranties.

Likelihood of Event	Action
Probable	Recognize the liability and disclose.
Reasonably Possible	Disclose only.
	No action required.

Example: A company estimates that its warranty claims will cost $750 during the current year. It recognizes the warranty liability when it makes the sale.

dr. Warranty Expense	$	750
dr. Warranty Liability	$	750

The company would only record the liability on the balance sheet if the event was reasonably probable.

Ratios and Turnover Metrics

Let alone key financial ratios of liquidity and efficiency, the proper management of current assets and liabilities directly impacts.

Ratio	Formula
Current Ratio	Current Assets ÷ Current Liabilities
Quick Ratio	(Cash + Receivables + Short-Term Investments) ÷ Current Liabilities

Turnover Metrics: Turnover measures how efficiently a company manages its assets.

Metric	Formula
Accounts Receivable Turnover	Net Sales ÷ Average Accounts Receivable
Inventory Turnover	Cost of

Conclusion

Short term financial stability relies on current monetary assets and liabilities. The core challenge is going to be in managing these components: cash and receivables, payroll and warranties, etc., to maintain liquidity, optimize cash flow and prevent risk. This chapter not only explained the significance of precisely watching and producing these accounts, liabilities but also brought rise to the strategic information that can develop a company's finance management exercises. In light of that, whether determining the complexities of bad debt, applying receivables for financing or accounting for contingent liabilities, each decision has significant impact on a firm's financial health. Next, in the next chapter, we investigate how to strategically manage inventory so as to balance stock levels to meet demand but without overloading their resources.

CHAPTER 7
TIME VALUE, NOTES AND BONDS

Those companies engaged in financing activities involving notes and bonds need to understand the time value of money. Time value is the idea that today's one dollar is worth more than a dollar in the future because a dollar can generate income. This chapter also explored how to make present and future value calculations, how to consider notes payable, and how to manage bonds payable with specifics of bond discounts and bonds premiums.

Time Value of Money

Time value of money (TVM) is a basic financial concept, which states that money available now can be invested to earn a return and will therefore have value greater than the same amount in the future. We use TVM calculations to value both lump sums and annuities over time.

Formula for Future Value	Formula for Present Value
$FV = PV \times (1 + i)^n$	$PV = FV \div (1 + i)^n$
$FV = PV \times TVMF$	$PV = FV \times TVMF$

Where:

- **i** = Interest rate per period
- **n** = Number of periods
- **TVMF** = Time value of money factor, often found in TVM tables

Example: To calculate the present value of a $20 payment to be made 10 years from now with an interest rate of 4%, use the formula:

PV = $20 ÷ (1 + 0.04)^10 = $13.51

Strategic Insight: An understanding of the time value of money enables businesses to assess deferred cash flow costs for better financial decision making. For example, it determines whether it should accept payments over time or demand upfront cash.

Notes Payable

Notes Payable represent obligations to pay a specified sum of money on a future date, often with interest. Notes can be serial or term, depending on whether payments are made periodically or in one lump sum.

Key Definitions	Explanation
Serial Notes Payable	Periodic payments that cover both principal and interest.
Term Notes Payable	Payment of the principal in full at the note's maturity date.

Example: A company issues a $100,000 note payable with a 5-year term and a 6% market interest rate. The present value of the periodic payments can be calculated using the PVA (present value of an annuity) formula:

PVA = $100,000 × 4.21236 = $23,739.66 (annual payment amount)

The journal entries to record the note and subsequent payments are as follows:

1/1/1:

dr. Cash	$ 100,000
cr. Notes Payable	$ 100,000

12/31/1:

dr. Interest Expense	$ 6,000
cr. Notes Payable	$ 17,739.66
cr. Cash	$ 23,739.66

Strategic Insight: Managing notes payable effectively can improve a company's cash flow by allowing it to defer large cash outflows and match payments with incoming cash from operations.

Bonds Payable

Bonds Payable represent long-term borrowing, where the company issues debt to raise funds from investors. Bonds may be **term bonds** (mature in full on a single date) or **serial** bonds (mature in installments over time).

Term	Explanation
Bond Discount	Occurs when bonds are issued for less than their face value.
Bond Premium	Occurs when bonds are issued for more than their face value.

Example: A company issues $10,000 bonds payable at a discount. The bonds have a face value of $10,000, an 8% coupon rate, and semiannual interest payments. The market interest rate is 6%.

The present value of the principal and interest payments is calculated as follows:

PV of Principal = $10,000 × 0.74409 = $7,440.90

PV of Interest Payments = $400 × 8.5302 = $3,412.08

Total PV = $7,440.90 + $3,412.08 = $10,852.98

The journal entries for issuing the bonds and subsequent interest payments are:

1/1:

Cash	$ 10,852.98
cr. Bonds Payable	$ 10,000
cr. Bonds Premium	$ 852.98

7/1:

dr. Interest Expence	$ 325.59
cr. Bond Premium	$ 74.41
cr. Cash	$ 400

Strategic Insight: Bonds offer companies a way to secure long-term financing at potentially lower interest rates than bank loans. The use of bond discounts and premiums reflects market conditions and can affect a company's overall cost of capital.

Effective Interest Method for Amortization

The **Effective Interest Method** is the preferred method for amortizing bond discounts and premiums because it matches interest expense with the carrying amount of the bond over time. Under this method, the interest expense in each period is calculated by multiplying the bond carrying value by the market interest rate.

Example: For a bond issued at a premium, the interest expense decreases over time as the bond carrying value approaches its face value. The journal entry for interest payments reflects this decrease:

1/1:

dr. Interest Expence	$ 325.59
cr. Bond Premium	$ 74.41
cr. Cash	$ 400

Strategic Insight: Using the effective interest method ensures that interest expense reflects the true cost of borrowing over time, providing a more accurate measure of financial performance.

Non-Interest Bearing Notes

Non-interest bearing notes do not explicitly state an interest rate but are issued at a discount, which effectively includes interest in the repayment terms. The difference between the amount borrowed and the amount repaid is the implied interest.

Example: A company issues a $5,000 non-interest bearing note. The implied interest is recognized over the life of the note:

1/1:

dr. Cash	$ 4.500
cr. Notes payable	$ 5,000

12/31:

dr. Interest Expense	$ 500
cr. Notes payable	$ 500

Strategic Insight: Non-interest bearing notes allow companies to borrow at a lower upfront cost, but the implied interest must be carefully managed to avoid unexpected expenses down the road.

Bond Issuance Costs

Bond Issuance Costs include legal, accounting, and underwriting fees related to issuing bonds. These costs are treated as a reduction in the carrying value of the bond and are amortized over the bond's life.

Example: A company issues bonds with $100 in bond issuance costs. The journal entry records these costs as a deduction from the bond's value:

1/1:

dr. Cash	$ 9,900
cr. Bond issuance Costs	$ 100
dr. Bonds Payable	$ 10,000

Strategic Insight: Amortization of bond issuance costs makes the matching of expenses with periods of generating benefit more precise by spreading bond issuance expenses over the life of the bond.

Conclusion

The ability to understand the time value of money, notes payable, and bonds payable is important for effective management of a company's financing activities. While these concepts can be applied properly, they can be used well by companies to optimize its debt structures, manage interest expenses, and improve its ability to plan financially. Companies can decide on borrowing, investing and raising capital through bonds by calculating present and future values.

CHAPTER 8
DEBT RESTRUCTURING TECHNIQUES

Debt restructuring is the process of restructuring of the outstanding debt of a business so as to lessen the burden of repayment of that debt. So, companies can restructure debt to reduce the interest rate, its payment terms or the amount they owe. The debtor can initiate restructuring voluntarily or these can be achieved as part of a formal bankruptcy process. The techniques of debt restructuring are explored in this chapter and the consequences for both debtors and creditors are discussed.

Debt Restructuring Methods

Debt restructuring can be categorized into two primary methods:

1. **Debt Settlement:** This method is one in which the creditor agrees to accept a less than the amount owed by the debtor from on settlement of the debt. Forgiveness can mean part of the principal, interest or both. The settlement itself is a gain to the debtor equal to the difference between the carrying value of the debt and the settlement amount.

2. **Modification of Terms**: In this method, debtor's payments are lowered in terms by interest rate or maturity date. Depending on the case at hand, the creditor may still get the full amount owed (or something close to it) but on a different schedule.

Example: The creditor will forgive $5,000 of a $50,000 note receivable and $2,000 of accrued interest with a carrying value of $40,000 on the creditor's books. The journal entries for the debt settlement are as follows:

1/1/3:

dr. Land	$ 40,000
cr. Notes Receivable	$ 50,000
dr. Interest Receivable	$ 2,000
cr. Gain on Settlement	$ 12,000

In contrast, if the creditor agrees to modify the terms of the note by reducing the interest rate and extending the maturity, the debtor records a gain on modification if the carrying value exceeds the total future cash payments under the new terms.

Modification of Terms: Debtor's Perspective

When a debt carrying value is greater than the total future cash payments (including both principal and interest) under modified terms, the debtor recognizes a gain on the modification. The gain is calculated as the difference between the carrying value of the debt and the present value of the modified cash flows.

Example: A company restructures a $22,000 note payable, reducing the interest rate to 5% and extending the maturity. The new terms result in total future cash payments of $21,000. The journal entries to record the modification are:

1/1/11:

dr. Notes Payable	$ 22,000
cr. Cash	$ 21,000
cr. Gain on Modification	$ 1,000

If the carrying value is less than the total future cash payments under the new terms, the debtor does not recognize a gain. Instead, the debtor continues to recognize interest expense using the effective interest method at the modified rate.

Example: A debtor restructures a $24,024 note payable with future cash payments of $22,000 and accrued interest of $2,024. The journal entry to record the interest expense and payment is as follows:

12/31/12:

dr. Interest Expense	$ 1,034
cr. Interest Payable	$ 1,034

12/31/13:

dr. Notes Payable	$ 22,000
dr. Interest Payable	$ 2,024
cr. Cash	$ 24,024

Debt Settlement

Debt settlement involves the partial or full forgiveness of debt, allowing the debtor to settle the obligation for less than its carrying value. This method typically occurs when the debtor is experiencing financial distress and is unable to meet the original terms of the debt agreement.

The creditor records a loss on the settlement equal to the difference between the carrying value of the receivable and the settlement amount received. For the debtor, the difference between the carrying value of the debt and the settlement amount is recognized as a gain.

Example: A debtor and creditor agree to settle a $50,000 note receivable and $2,000 of accrued interest for $40,000. The journal entries to record the settlement on the creditor's books are as follows:

1/1/3:

dr. Land	$ 40,000
dr. Loss on Settlement	$ 12,000
dr. Notes Receivable	$ 50,000
cr. Interest Receivable	$ 2,000

For the debtor:

1/1/3:

dr. Notes Payable	$ 50,000
dr. Interest Payable	$ 2,000
dr. Cash	$ 40,000
cr. Gain on Settlement	$ 12,000

Debt settlement provides immediate relief for the debtor, allowing them to reduce their overall debt burden. However, it may also have significant tax implications, as the gain recognized by the debtor could be considered taxable income.

Modification of Terms: Creditor's Perspective

From the creditor's perspective, a modification of terms typically results in a remeasurement of the receivable based on the present value of the modified cash flows, discounted at the original effective interest rate. If the present value of the modified payments is less than the carrying value of the receivable, the creditor recognizes a loss on the modification.

Example: A creditor restructures a $24,024 note receivable with modified future payments totaling $22,000. The present value of the modified payments at the original rate of 6% is $21,975. The creditor records a loss on modification as follows:

12/31/12:

dr. Interest Receivable	$ 1,034
cr. Interest Income	$ 1,034

12/31/13:

dr. Loss on Modification	$ 49
dr. Cash	$ 22,000
cr. Notes Receivable	$ 21,975
cr. Interest Receivable	$ 1,034

For the creditor, restructuring the debt may result in a reduction in expected cash flows and a corresponding loss. However, restructuring may also allow the creditor to recover a portion of the debt that might otherwise have gone unpaid.

Strategic Insights into Debt Restructuring

For the distressed companies, debt restructuring presents both opportunities and challenges. This restructuring can help eliminate excessive debt consumption and cash flow and whether bankruptcy can be stayed. Yet restructuring can result in the recognition of gains or losses that can have tax implications and impact a company's reported financial performance.

If restructuring is successful, it allows creditors to recover some of the debt, rather than writing it off as uncollectible. Creditor may prevent larger losses and keep the relationship for future transactions by working with the debtor to change debt terms.

Strategic Considerations:

1. **Debtor's Perspective:** Companies must assess whether restructuring will be enough to relieve their financial situation for better. Debt modification or settlement gain recognized improves the balance sheet balance but also adds tax liability.

2. **Creditor's Perspective:** Creditors should take a step back to see if they'd get better recovery by modifying the terms of the debt in terms of where recovery is concerned rather than having the debtor defaulted. If re-negotiated new terms are discussed, creditors can salvage some of the outstanding receivables.

Conclusion

Debt restructuring techniques give firms a way of coping with financial distress without defaulting and sending bankruptcy. Restructuring can either take the form of debt settlement or renegotiation of terms, and leaves both debtors and creditors better off. Yet these actions carry hefty financial reporting and tax consequences and will need to be weighed carefully by both parties.

In the next chapter, we will delve deeper into advanced financial instruments utilized in corporate finance, such as derivatives, hedging strategies, and the part they play in managing risk.

CHAPTER 9
LEASE ACCOUNTING

Lease accounting is important to financial reporting because companies with assets do not have to own them, but can manage and control them. Leases can be classified into two categories: Finance Leases and Operating Leases. Each classification through accounting is different and affects a company's balance sheet, income statement and financial ratios. This chapter considers the criteria for lease classification, the treatment for each class of lease, and the repercussions for the lessees.

Lease Classification Criteria

Accounting is done based on several criteria and this is determined by how you think of lease association. If a lease meets one or more of the following criteria, it is classified as a Finance Lease (otherwise known as a capital lease):

1. **Transfer of Ownership:** The lease transfers ownership of the asset to the lessee by the end of the lease term.

2. **Purchase Option:** The lease grants the lessee an option to purchase the asset at a price sufficiently lower than the fair value, indicating that exercise is reasonably certain.

3. **Lease Term:** The lease term is for a major part of the economic life of the asset.

4. **Present Value:** The present value of lease payments equals or exceeds substantially all of the fair value of the leased asset.

5. **Specialized Asset:** The asset is of such a specialized nature that only the lessee can use it without major modifications.

If none of these criteria are met, the lease is classified as an **Operating Lease.**

Example: A lessee enters into a lease for equipment with a fair value of $16,000, a residual value of $2,000, and an economic life of 9 years. The lease term is 3 years, and the present value of lease payments is calculated as follows:

PV of Lease Payments = $5,054 (annual lease payment)

Accounting for Operating Leases

For operating leases, the lessee records both **a right-of-use asset** and a **lease liability** on the balance sheet. The lease liability is measured at the present value of future lease payments, while the right-of-use asset is amortized over the lease term.

Example: On 1/1/1, a lessee leases an asset with a right-of-use value of $14,321. The journal entries for the initial recognition and subsequent lease payments are as follows:

1/1/1:

dr. Right-of-Use Asset	$	14,321
cr. Lease Liability	$	14,321

1/1/1:

dr. Lease Liability	$	5,054
cr. Cash	$	5,054

12/31/1:

dr. Lease Expense	$	5,054
cr. Lease Liability	$	5,054

The lease expense is recognized on a straight-line basis over the lease term, and the liability is reduced as payments are made.

Accounting for Finance Leases

Finance leases (formerly capital leases) require the lessee to recognize both a right-of-use asset and a lease liability. The key difference between a finance lease and an operating lease is the recognition of **interest expense** and **amortization expense.**

In a finance lease, the lessee amortizes the right-of-use asset over the shorter of the lease term or the asset's useful life. Interest expense is calculated using the effective interest method, whereby interest is recognized on the lease liability over time.

Example: The lessee enters a finance lease with a right-of-use asset of $14,321 and annual lease payments of $5,054. The effective interest method is used to amortize the lease liability, resulting in the following journal entries:

1/1/1:

dr. Right-of-Use Asset	$	14,321
Cr. Lease Liability	$	14,321

1/1/1:

dr. Lease Liability	$	5,054
Cash	$	5,054

12/31/1:

dr. Interest Expense	$	556
dr. Lease Liabiity	$	4,498
cr. Cash	$	5,054

12/31/1:

dr. Amortization Expense	$	2,864
Cr. Right-of-Use Asset	$	2,864

As seen above, interest expense decreases over time as the lease liability is reduced, while amortization expense remains consistent throughout the lease term.

Effective Interest Method for Lease Liability

Both operating and finance leases use the **effective interest method** to amortize the lease liability. However, the difference between the two lies in the recognition of expenses:

- **Operating Lease:** The lessee records lease expense on a straight-line basis over the lease term.
- **Finance Lease:** The lessee records both interest expense and amortization expense, resulting in a front-loaded expense pattern.

Example: A company leases an asset for three years and calculates the annual lease payment as $5,054. The effective interest table shows the interest and amortization breakdown over the lease term:

Year 1:

  Interest Expense = $556

  Decrease in Lease Liability = $4,498

  Remaining Lease Liability = $9,267

This pattern continues until the lease liability is fully amortized by the end of the lease term.

Disclosures for Leases

Lessee companies are required to disclose key information about their lease obligations in the financial statements. These disclosures include:

1. **Future Lease Payments:** Disclose the total amount of lease payments expected over the next five years, along with the total remaining obligation.

2. **Residual Value Guarantees:** If the lessee guarantees the residual value of the leased asset, any excess liability must be recognized on the balance sheet.

Example: A residual value guarantee maintains that the residual value of a leased asset cannot fall below $2,000. If the residual value is estimated to be $1,500, the lessee needs to add a liability for the $500 shortfall.

Strategic Insights into Lease Accounting

More than financial reporting, lease accounting has an impact on a company's financial ratios, debt covenants, and decision making process. For example:

- **Leverage Ratios:** Operating leases now require the recognition of both assets and liabilities on the balance sheet, which may increase a company's debt-to-equity ratio and affect loan covenants.
- **Expense Patterns:** Expenses from finance leases are front loaded, whereas expenses from operating leases are straight lined. The companies then need to choose which lease classification is more advantageous from a financial perspective.

For companies who want to control valuable assets while avoiding large upfront investment, leasing still is a good option. A company's strategic and financial goals, as well as accounting, will determine the choice between an operating lease and a finance lease.

Conclusion

With the new lease accounting standards, companies must now recognize and report leases on their financial statements differently than before. Regardless of whether the lease is classified as an operating lease or a finance lease, companies must carefully evaluate terms and conditions of each lease to determine proper accounting treatment and disclosure. Furthermore, a company can make or break on strategic decisions regarding lease classification, given that both can have considerable impact on financial performance and operational flexibility.

The next chapter deals with the advanced topics, such as sale-leaseback transactions and their accounting implications.

CHAPTER 10
TAXATION IN ACCOUNTING

Our accounting system relies on taxation which affects financial statements of companies and individuals alike. Deferred tax liabilities or assets are recognized on the balance sheet because of differences between GAAP accounting and tax rules. Temporary and permanent differences between accounting income and taxable income give rise to these deferred tax items. This chapter examines how to take into account these differences and the effects of taxes that are deferred into the future on financial reporting.

Deferred Tax Liabilities and Assets

Future tax obligations or benefits arising from differences between financial reporting and tax reporting amounts and their reconciliation, referred to as differences or deferred tax assets and liabilities. All of these will reverse eventually though and will cause you to have additional tax payments (deferred tax liability) or reduced tax (deferred tax asset) in future periods.

Tax Formulas	Explanation
Deferred Tax Liability = Net Temporary Difference × Tax Rate	Represents taxes owed in the future due to temporary differences.
Income Tax Payable = Taxable Income × Tax Rate	Taxes currently due based on taxable income as reported on the tax return.
Income Tax Expense = Income Tax Payable + Deferred Tax Liability	Total tax expense recognized in the financial statements, including current and future taxes.

Example: Assume a company owes total income taxes of $25,000 in 20X1 due to business operations. Of this, $20,000 must be paid in 20X2 according to tax law. In this case, the company will record a **deferred tax liability** of $5,000 in 20X1, recognizing the future tax payment.

Temporary Differences

Temporary differences are differences between the tax basis of an asset or liability and its reported amount in the financial statements. These differences are expected to reverse in the future, resulting in deferred tax liabilities or assets.

Examples of Temporary Differences
Accrual Method vs. Cash Method: Income is recognized on the accrual basis in accounting but taxed on a cash basis.
Depreciation Differences: GAAP may use straight-line depreciation, while tax rules may allow accelerated depreciation.

Example: A company uses the straight-line depreciation method for GAAP reporting but uses accelerated depreciation for tax purposes. As a result, the company records higher depreciation expenses for tax purposes in the early years of an asset's life, creating a temporary difference.

Journal Entry Example:

In 20X1, the company had GAAP pretax income of $100,000, with a temporary difference of $10,000 due to accelerated depreciation for tax purposes, leading to taxable income of $90,000. The tax rate is 40%. The journal entry to record the income tax expense is as follows:

12/31/1:

dr. Income Tax Expense	$ 40,000
cr. Income Tax Payable	$ 36,000
cr. Deferred Tax Liability	$ 4,000

In 20X2, the temporary difference reverses, increasing taxable income to $110,000. The journal entry is adjusted accordingly:

12/31/2:

dr. Income Tax Expense	$ 40,000
cr. Deferred Tax Liability	$ 4,000
cr. Income Tax Payable	$ 44,000

Strategic Insight: Temporary differences can significantly affect a company's cash flow and tax strategy. By carefully managing the timing of income and deductions, companies can defer taxes and retain more cash for investment in operations or other business activities.

Permanent Differences

Permanent differences are differences between taxable income and accounting income that will never reverse. These differences do not create deferred tax liabilities or assets and do not affect future taxable income.

> **Examples of Permanent Differences**
>
> **Tax-Exempt Interest:** Interest from state and municipal bonds is exempt from federal taxes but still included in GAAP income.
>
> **Non-Deductible Expenses:** Expenses such as fines, penalties, or life insurance premiums for executives may be recognized for accounting purposes but are not deductible for tax purposes.

Example: When a company generates $5,000 of tax exempt interest from municipal bonds, that income is reported on the financial statements, but not in the taxable income determination.

Permanent differences are not included in the deferred tax accounts but they do affect the rate of the effective tax which may be different from the statutory tax for the exclusion or inclusion of certain of the income or of expenses.

Strategic Insight: Permanent differences helps the management understand that some work will have an effect on both on the accounting as well as tax obligations. Often, these differences can result in tax planning opportunities for tax exempt investments or non deductible expenses.

Income Tax Expense Calculation

Income tax expense is a calculation based both on current taxes payable on taxable income and deferred taxes associated with temporary differences.

GAAP Income	Taxable Income
20X1: $120,000	20X1: $ 90,000
20X2: $120,000	20X2: $110,000

Due to the differences in income based on depreciation methods the company must account for deferred taxes and the current taxes. This shows through the total income tax expense, which brings together both the taxes payable and the deferred tax liabilities.

Strategic Insight: The income tax expense is directly related to a company's net income. Companies must analyze current and deferred tax accounts carefully to represent the company's financial position in an accurate manner. This also brings out the necessity of temporary differences and how they can be used to implement tax deferral strategies.

Conclusion

Financial reporting and strategic decision making takes place with tax accounting in place. To manage deferred tax liabilities and assets and permanent differences, companies need to know the differences between GAAP and tax rules. The correctness of accounting not only for current but also for deferred taxes is important for companies to properly present their financial performance and also to maximize the tax efficiency. The following chapter outlines other advanced tax planning strategies, their impact on corporate financial structures, an overview of using tax shelters, and the use of international tax planning techniques.

CHAPTER 11
EQUITY AND STOCKHOLDERS' RIGHTS

Residual Interest in the Assets of the Company after the deduction of liabilities constitutes Equity. Common stock and preferred stock divide equity among stockholders, each with its own rights and obligations. To understand equity and stockholders rights plays a vital role in corporate governance and financial management. This chapter looks at the basics of equity, stock trading, distribution of dividends, and the privileges associated with different types of stock.

Common Stock and Preferred Stock

Stockholders' equity consists of two primary components: **common stock** and **preferred stock.** Common stockholders typically hold voting rights and share in the company's profits through dividends. Preferred stockholders, on the other hand, usually do not have voting rights but have priority in dividend distribution and liquidation.

Common Stock Rights	Preferred Stock Rights
Voting rights (e.g., director elections)	Priority in dividend distribution
Share in dividends after preferred stock	Priority in liquidation over common stock
Share in liquidation after preferred stock	Usually no voting rights

Types of Preferred Stock

Preferred stock can be customized to meet the needs of both the corporation and its investors. There are several types of preferred stock, each offering different benefits and obligations:

- **Participating:** Stockholders share in additional dividends with common stockholders after preferred dividends are paid.

- **Cumulative:** Stockholders are entitled to receive dividends in arrears if they are not paid in a given year.

- **Convertible:** Stockholders can convert preferred shares into common shares at a predetermined ratio.

- **Redeemable:** The corporation must repurchase the shares at a fixed price in the future, which creates a liability on the balance sheet.

Example: A corporation issues redeemable preferred stock, which must be repurchased after five years. The corporation treats this stock as a liability due to the mandatory redemption.

Stock Issuance and Subscription

When a corporation issues common or preferred stock, it receives cash in exchange for shares. The accounting entries for stock issuance are relatively straightforward:

Example: A company issues common stock for $15 per share, with a $10 par value. The journal entry is as follows:

dr. Cash	$	15
cr. Common Stock	$	10
cr. Paid-in Capital Common Stock	$	5

In some cases, companies allow investors to subscribe to stock by paying in installments. Stock subscriptions create a **subscription receivable,** which is recorded as **contra equity** until the payment is complete.

Example: A company receives partial payment for a stock subscription. The journal entry is as follows:

dr. Cash	$	7,500
Cr. Common Stock Subscribed	$	7,500

Once the full payment is received and the stock is issued, the final entry is recorded:

dr. Common Stock Subscribed	$	7,500
cr. Common Stock	$	7,500

Treasury Stock

Treasury stock is stock that a company has repurchased from its shareholders. It is recorded as **contra equity** and reduces the total stockholders' equity on the balance sheet.

Treasury stock can be accounted for using the **cost method** or the **par value method.** The **cost method** records the purchase of treasury stock at the price paid by the company, while the **par value method** records treasury stock at its original par value.

Example (Cost Method): A company repurchases 100 shares of its common stock at $22 per share. The journal entry is:

dr. Treasury Stock	$	2,200
cr. Cash	$	2,200

When the company later reissues the stock at $25 per share, the journal entry is:

dr. Cash	$	2,500
cr. Treasury Stock	$	2,200
cr. Paid-in Capital - Trreasury Stock	$	300

Dividend Allocation

Corporations distribute profits to stockholders in the form of dividends. Dividends can be classified as:

1. **Dividends in Arrears:** Unpaid dividends on cumulative preferred stock, which must be paid before common stockholders receive any dividends.

2. **Current Year Dividends:** Dividends declared during the current year.

3. **Participating Dividends:** Additional dividends paid to preferred stockholders if certain conditions are met.

Example: A corporation declares a total of $40,000 in dividends. The company owes two years of dividends in arrears to preferred stockholders and must distribute the remaining amount to common stockholders.

Cumulative, Non-Participating	Cumulative, Participating
Preferred Dividends: $15,000	Preferred Dividends: $25,789
Common Dividends: $25,000	Common Dividends: $14,211

The allocation of dividends depends on whether the preferred stock is **participating** or **non-participating**. Participating preferred stockholders are entitled to share in excess dividends after common stockholders receive their share.

Stock Dividends and Splits

Stock dividends distribute additional shares to shareholders rather than cash. Stock dividends increase the number of outstanding shares while decreasing the earnings per share, but they do not affect total equity.

Stock splits increase the number of shares outstanding and reduce the par value per share. A stock split does not affect total equity but makes shares more affordable and accessible to investors.

Example: A company declares a 2-for-1 stock split, doubling the number of shares outstanding and halving the par value of each share. No journal entry is required for a stock split, but it affects the number of shares and the par value in the equity section of the balance sheet.

Retained Earnings

Retained earnings represent the cumulative profits of a company that have not been distributed as dividends. Retained earnings can be **appropriated** (set aside for a specific purpose) **or unappropriated** (available for general use).

Example: A company appropriates retained earnings to finance a future stock buyback. The journal entry is as follows:

dr. Retained Earnings	$ 100,000
cr. Appropriated Retained Earning	$ 2,200

Quasi-Reorganization

A **quasi-reorganization** allows a company to eliminate a deficit in retained earnings without going through formal bankruptcy proceedings. The company revalues its assets, reduces the par value of its stock, and transfers paid-in capital to offset the deficit.

Example: A company writes down overvalued assets and uses the resulting reduction to eliminate its retained earnings deficit. The journal entry is:

dr. Retained Earnings	$ 50,000
cr. Asset Write-Down	$ 50,000

Stock Option Plans

Stock option plans give employees the right to purchase company stock at a predetermined price, typically as a form of compensation. These options are recorded as **compensation expense** over the vesting period.

Example: A company grants stock options to employees with an exercise price of $20 per share. The value of the options is recorded as compensation expense:

dr. Compensation Expense	$ 40,000
cr. Paid-in Capital – Stock Options	$ 40,000

When the options are exercised, the company records the following:

dr. Cash	$ 200,000
cr. Paid-in Capital – Stock Options	$ 40,000
cr. Common Stock	$ 240,000

Corporate Bankruptcy

In the event of corporate bankruptcy, assets are distributed to creditors and stockholders based on their priority:

1. **Creditors with Priority:** These creditors receive payment first, ahead of secured creditors.

2. **Fully Secured Creditors:** These creditors receive payment from assets pledged as collateral.

3. **Partially Secured Creditors:** These creditors receive partial payment from pledged assets.

4. **Unsecured Creditors:** These creditors receive payment from any remaining assets.

Example: A company in bankruptcy must distribute its assets in order of priority, starting with secured creditors and working down to unsecured creditors.

Conclusion

Corporate Governance and Financial Strategy are integral parts of equity and stockholders' rights. A company will grow better if it understands the difference between the various types of stock, the way in which a company allocates dividends, and how to account stock transactions. Also, corporations can critically use treasury stock, stock option plans and retained earnings to create accepted value to shareholders while at the same time retaining the use of their financial resources.

We will explore in the next chapter advanced tradeoffs in corporate finance such as mergers and acquisitions and capital restructuring to further improve stockholder value.

CHAPTER 12
EARNINGS PER SHARE ANALYSIS

Earnings Per Share (EPS) is one of the most used metric in financial analysis and reporting. EPS indicates that profit per share is an important measure of a company's profitability which give an indication of how much money each common shareholder receives. All public companies are required to present EPS of income from continuing operations and net income on face of income statement under GAAP. This chapter shows how to calculate basic and diluted EPS, as well as the impact of different capital structures on EPS.

Capital Structures and EPS

How EPS is calculated depends on the structure of a company's capital. Depending on the complexity of the capital structure, either only Basic **EPS**, or Basic **EPS** and Diluted EPS are reported.

1. **Simple Capital Structure:** A simple capital structure company issues only common stock, and does not have potentially dilutive securities such as convertible preferred stock or stock options. Basic EPS is reported by companies with simple capital structure.

2. **Complex Capital Structure:** Potentially dilutive securities (e.g., convertible preferred stock, options, or convertible bonds) are included in a complex capital structure. Companies with a complex capital structure must report both Basic **EPS** and **Diluted EPS.**

Basic EPS Calculation

Basic EPS is the most straightforward measure of earnings per share, representing the net income available to common shareholders divided by the weighted average number of common shares outstanding during the period.

Formula:

Basic EPS = (Net Income - Current Year Preferred Dividends) ÷ Weighted Average Common Shares Outstanding (WACS)

To calculate **Basic EPS,** you must first account for any **current year cumulative preferred dividends,** whether or not they have been declared. These dividends are subtracted from **net income** before dividing by the **weighted average common shares outstanding (WACS).**

Example: Consider a company with the following activities:

- **Shares Outstanding:** The company starts with 75,000 shares at the beginning of the year.
- **New Shares Issued:** The company issues 60,000 new shares during the year.
- **5% Stock Dividend:** The company issues a 5% stock dividend, increasing the total shares.
- **Repurchased Shares:** The company repurchases 10,000 shares during the year.

To calculate WACS:

WACS = 131,250 shares (including the stock dividend) - 2,500 (repurchased shares) + 1,000 (treasury shares reissued)

WACS = 129,750 shares

The Basic EPS calculation would then divide the net income (minus preferred dividends) by the WACS.

Diluted EPS Calculation

Diluted EPS accounts for the potential dilution of earnings that could occur if all **convertible securities** - such as convertible bonds, stock options, or convertible preferred stock—were converted into common stock. This provides a more conservative measure of EPS, assuming the maximum possible dilution.

Formula:

Diluted EPS = (Net Income + Adjusted Bond Interest Expense Net of Tax) ÷ (WACS + Potential Common Stock from Dilutive Securities)

When calculating diluted EPS, assume that all dilutive securities are converted into common shares at the beginning of the year, or when the securities are issued, if later. This increases the denominator by the number of potential common shares.

Example: The company has convertible preferred stock that could be converted into common shares. In this case, you would adjust the numerator by adding back any bond interest expense (net of tax) that would no longer be incurred if the bonds were converted into common stock. The denominator increases by the number of shares that could be issued upon conversion.

Key Points for Diluted EPS:

- **Numerator Adjustments:** If preferred stock is convertible into common stock, then preferred dividends are not subtracted from net income.

- **Denominator Adjustments:** Contingent shares are included in the denominator if the conditions for their issuance are met.

Diluted EPS cannot be higher than Basic EPS, as the dilution reduces the earnings attributable to each share. In the event of a net loss, Diluted EPS is set equal to Basic EPS because it cannot be lower.

Impact of Stock Dividends and Splits

When calculating EPS, you must adjust the weighted average number of shares outstanding for **stock dividends** and **stock splits.** These adjustments are applied retroactively to all periods presented in the financial statements, even if the dividend or split occurred after the period ended but before the financial statements were issued.

Example: A company declares a 5% stock dividend after the year-end but before the financial statements are issued. The number of shares is adjusted as though the dividend had occurred at the beginning of the year, increasing the weighted average common shares outstanding.

Strategic Insights on EPS

EPS helps investors understand a company's profitability and through that the ability to make informed decisions. EPS is often used by analysts to track management's success at making profits for shareholders over time. All of these, however, don't give us a complete picture. Overall, analysts will view a company's financial health as just a portion of the whole picture, taking into consideration variables like revenue growth, profit margins and cash flow, along with that.

While Basic EPS is an important indicator for shareholders, **Diluted EPS** offers a more conservative and realistic view of possible earnings per share for companies with complex capital structures. For instance, securities such as convertible bonds, stock options and warrants can have a dilutive impact and reduce the amount of earnings available to shareholders in the future.

Conclusion

Earnings Per Share (EPS) is one of the most important measures of a company's profitability and financial performance. The ability to calculate and interpret EPS in different ways (Basic EPS vs Diluted EPS) is important for both management and shows how investors look at it. Basic EPS is reported from a company with simple capital structure while Diluted EPS is reported from a company with complex capital structure. EPS calculation and report are accurate so that stakeholders know what a company's earnings potential is.

In the next chapter we will discuss advanced financial ratios and how they help evaluate the performance of a company beyond just EPS.

CHAPTER 13
INVESTMENT ACCOUNTING

The area of **investment accounting** is a key area that factored in how companies report their financial investments in other entities. Companies can acquire other firms' equity or debt securities for various reasons – to earn returns or to gain control in another business. All of these investments are accounted for using the method determining the level of control or influence the investor has over the investor, the classification of the investment and whether it is held as an investment for trading, sale, or maturity.

Investment Classifications

Investments in debt and equity securities are classified into three primary categories:

1. **Trading Securities:** These are investments that a company intends to hold for the short term with the objective of buying and selling for profit. Trading securities are recorded at **fair value,** with unrealized gains or losses recognized directly in **net income.**

2. **Available-for-Sale Securities:** These investments are neither classified as trading nor held-to-maturity securities. They are recorded at **fair value,** but unlike trading securities, unrealized gains and losses are reported in **other comprehensive income (OCI)** until they are realized upon sale.

3. **Held-to-Maturity Securities:** Debt securities that the company intends to hold until maturity are classified as held-to-maturity. These are recorded at **amortized cost**, and unrealized gains or losses are not recognized.

Accounting for Debt Investments

Debt securities represent a creditor relationship and can be classified as **held-to-maturity, trading,** or **available-for-sale.** The accounting treatment differs based on the classification.

Example (Held-to-Maturity): A company purchases $1,000 of debt securities at a discount, expecting to hold them until maturity. The journal entry to record the purchase would be:

dr. Debt Investment	$	1,000
cr. Cash	$	900
cr. Discount	$	100

As the company receives interest, it recognizes interest income and amortizing the discount over time.

Example (Trading Securities): A company purchases $1,000 of debt securities classified as trading securities. If the fair value increases by $300, the company recognizes the gain in net income:

| dr. Fair Value Adjustment | $ | 300 |
| cr. Unrealized Gain – Income | $ | 300 |

Upon sale, the realized gain or loss is recorded in net income.

Accounting for Equity Investments

Equity investments represent an ownership interest in another entity, and the accounting treatment depends on the investor's level of influence:

1. **Fair Value Method:** Used when the investor owns less than 20% of the voting stock and has no significant influence over the investee. These investments are recorded at **fair value,** with unrealized gains and losses recognized in **net income.**

2. **Equity Method:** Applied when the investor owns between 20% and 50% of the voting stock, giving them significant influence over the investee. Under the equity method, the investor recognizes their share of the investee's profits or losses in their own financial statements.

3. **Consolidation:** If the investor owns more than 50% of the voting stock, the investee is considered a subsidiary, and the investor consolidates the investee's financial statements with their own.

Fair Value Method

Under the fair value method, companies recognize investments at their fair value. Any changes in the fair value are recognized through income.

Example: A company purchases $1,000 of equity securities. If the fair value increases by $300, the company recognizes an unrealized gain in net income:

dr. Fair Value Adjustment	$	300
cr. Unrealized Gain - Income	$	300

Similarly, dividends received from the investee are recorded as dividend income:

dr. Cash	$	50
cr. Dividend Income	$	50

Equity Method

The equity method is used when the investor has significant influence over the investee, usually represented by ownership of between 20% and 50% of the voting stock.

Under the equity method, the investor's share of the investee's net income increases the carrying value of the investment, while dividends received reduce it.

Example: A company buys 25% of another company's stock for $20,000. During the year, the investee reports net income of $2,000 and declares dividends of $400. The investor's share of the income and dividends is recorded as follows:

Under the equity method, the investor recognizes their share of the investee's net income or loss and adjusts the carrying value of the investment accordingly. Dividends received from the investee reduce the carrying value of the investment rather than being recognized as income, as the equity method views dividends as a return on investment rather than revenue.

Recording the Investor's Share of Income

When the investee reports income, the investor records their share of that income as an increase in the carrying amount of the investment.

Example: A company owns 25% of another company's stock, for which it paid $20,000. During the year, the investor reports net income of $2,000.

The journal entry to record the investor's share of the investee's net income would be:

dr. Equity Investment	$ 500
cr. Income from Equity Investment	$ 500

In this case, 25% of the investee's net income ($2,000 × 25%) is $500. This amount is added to the carrying value of the equity investment, and the income is recognized in the investor's income statement.

Recording Dividends under the Equity Method

When the investee declares dividends, the investor records a reduction in the carrying value of the equity investment rather than recognizing it as income.

Example: Continuing with the previous scenario, the investee declares dividends of $400. The investor's share of the dividends is 25%, or $100.

The journal entry to record the dividends would be:

dr. Cash	$ 100
cr. Equity Investment	$ 100

The cash received from the dividends increases the investor's cash balance but reduces the carrying value of the investment by the same amount, as dividends are considered a return of capital under the equity method.

Example Summary

Let's summarize the equity method entries for the entire period:

1. Investment Purchase:

dr. Equity Investment	$ 20,000
cr. Cash	$ 20,000

2. **Recording Share of Investee's Net Income:**

dr. Equity Investment	$ 500
cr. Income from Equity Investment	$ 500

3. **Recording Dividends:**

dr. Cash	$ 100
cr. Equity Investment	$ 500

By the end of the year, the carrying value of the equity investment would be the original investment amount plus the investor's share of income, minus the dividends received:

- Initial investment: $20,000

- Plus share of income: $500

- Minus dividends received: $100

Carrying Value of Equity Investment = $20,400

Conclusion

Investment accounting is a nuanced area that requires a thorough understanding of how different types of investments are classified and reported. Whether dealing with debt or equity securities, the accounting methods—ranging from fair value adjustments to the equity method—reflect the level of influence or control the investor has over the investor. For debt securities, classifications into trading, available-for-sale, or held-to-maturity determine whether gains and losses are recognized in net income, other comprehensive income, or deferred until maturity. For equity investments, the level of ownership dictates whether the fair value method, equity method, or consolidation is applied. Understanding these distinctions is essential for accurately reflecting an entity's financial position and performance, ensuring transparency and consistency in financial reporting.

CHAPTER 14
SIMULATED CASH METHOD

The **Simulated Cash Method** provides a practical framework for converting accrual-based financial statements to a cash-based approach. This method is commonly used when businesses need to estimate cash flow for decision-making purposes without having direct cash flow statements. The goal of the simulated cash method is to reflect cash-based transactions and determine the cash inflows and outflows, even though actual cash may not yet have been exchanged. This is often achieved by adjusting the accrual basis to approximate the cash basis of accounting.

Converting Accrual to Simulated Cash Basis

To convert financial statements from the accrual basis to the simulated cash basis, adjustments are made to account for the differences between recorded accrual transactions and the cash that was actually exchanged.

This process involves adjusting key components from the balance sheet and income statement to simulate what the cash-based amounts would have been. Key items that often need adjustments include accounts receivable, accounts payable, unearned revenue, inventory, and cost of goods sold. The changes in these accounts over a period are used to estimate the cash flows.

The simulated cash method typically starts with the **net** income from accrual-based statements, followed by adjustments for non-cash items and changes in working capital accounts to reflect cash inflows and outflows.

Example of Converting Accrual Basis to Cash Basis

Consider the following scenario:

- On 12/31/1, Co. has **accounts receivable** of $40,000 and **unearned fees** of $10,000.

- During 20X2, Co. collects $20,000 of receivables, decreases unearned fees by $5,000, and receives $50,000 in cash from customers.

Accrual to Cash Adjustments:

1. Start with accrual net income and adjust for changes in non-cash accounts.

2. For **accounts receivable**: If receivables decreased by $20,000, it indicates that cash has been collected. Therefore, add the decrease in receivables to the cash inflows.

3. For **unearned revenue**: If unearned revenue decreases by $5,000, it means the company earned revenue for which cash was received in a prior period. The decrease in unearned revenue is added to simulate the cash earned during the period.

Journal entries for converting from accrual to simulated cash method:

dr. Cash	$	20,000
Cash	$	5,000
cr. Unearned Revenue	$	5,000

In the above entries, the **cash** account is increased, simulating the cash collections, while accounts receivable and unearned revenue are adjusted to reflect the changes.

Accrual to Cash Adjustments for Key Accounts

Key accounts in the balance sheet that often require adjustments when converting from accrual to simulated cash basis include:

- **Accounts Receivable:** Reflects cash collections from customers.
- **Inventory:** Adjusts for the cash paid for inventory purchases during the period.
- **Accounts Payable:** Reflects cash outflows to suppliers for inventory or services.
- **Unearned Revenue:** Reflects revenue earned during the period that was collected in a prior period.
- **Cost of Goods Sold (COGS):** Adjusts for the cash-based cost of goods that were sold during the period.

Example 2: Simulating Cash Paid to Suppliers

In this scenario, **Co.** starts with accounts payable of $25,000 and inventory valued at $50,000. During 20X2, Co. pays $54,000 in cash to suppliers.

1. Adjust **accounts payable** to reflect cash payments made during the year.
2. Adjust **inventory** to reflect purchases and cash flows related to goods sold.

dr. Cost of Goods Sold	$	30,000
cr. Inventory	$	30,000

dr. Accounts Payable	$	25,000
cr. Cash	$	25,000

dr. Cash	$	54,000
cr. Accounts Payable	$	54,000

Simulated Cash Flow and Financial Statement Analysis

The **simulated** cash method allows companies to simulate cash flows without generating cash flow statements directly. It is most useful for internal planning and analysis such as budgeting and forecasting. By transforming income statement transactions into cash based amounts and analyzing changes in balance sheet accounts companies can understand their cash flow patterns better and make better decisions about liquidity and financing."

Conclusion

The **Simulated Cash Method** provides a way to understand cash flow – without creating full cash flow statements – that is invaluable to companies that need to know their cash flows. Businesses can get a better idea of their liquidity, and better cash flow control by adjusting accrual based financial statements to act as if they were the customers transaction. This method allows us to estimate cash inflows and outflows by focusing on our major adjustments to accounts receivable, accounts payable, unearned revenue and inventory.

We will look in the next chapter at advanced forecasting and managing cash flow techniques using historical data and projected future transactions, which are built on the foundation of the simulated cash method.

CHAPTER 15
CASH FLOW STATEMENT TECHNIQUES

The **Cash Flow Statement** is one vital financial document which helps stakeholders understand how cash is being injected and/or pulled out of a company during a certain period. The statement is divided into three main sections: on the side of operating activities, investing activities, financing activities. This chapter concentrates on preparing the cash flow statement, including Indirect Method and **Direct Method** in calculating cash flows from operating activities.

The cash flow statement primarily answers two key questions:

1. Where did the cash come from during the period?
2. How was the cash used during the period?

In this chapter, I will present in detail how to use the direct and indirect approaches to the operating activities section of the cash flow statement.

The Indirect Method

The **Indirect Method** begins with net income and makes adjustments for changes in non cash items and working capital, to arrive at net cash provided by or used by operating activities. Due to its connection of accrual based net income with cash based operations, this is the most commonly used method.

Steps in Preparing the Indirect Method:

1. **Start with Net Income:** Begin with the net income figure from the income statement.
2. **Adjust for Non-Cash Effects:** Add back non-cash expenses (e.g., depreciation, amortization) and subtract non-cash revenues.
3. **Adjust for Changes in Operating Assets and Liabilities**: Change for increases and decreases int operating assets (e.g., accounts receivable, inventory), liabilities (e.g. accounts payable, accrued liabilities).

Example: Consider the following information for ABC Corporation:

- Net income: $50,000
- Depreciation: $5,000
- Bond discount amortization: $200
- Increase in accounts receivable: $(6,000)
- Increase in income tax payable: $700

Journal Entry	
Net Income	$ 50,000
Adjustments for Non-Cash Effects:	
Depreciation	+ $ 5,000
Bond Discount Amortization	+ $ 200
Change in Operating Assets and Liabilities:	
Increase in Accounts Receivable	- $ 6,000
Increase in Income Tax Payable	+ $ 700
Net Cash Flow from Operating Activities	$ 49,900

On the other hand, this method adjusts cash from operating activities by the (add back) non-cash expenses (depreciation and amortization) and changes in the working capital accounts to get the net cash provided by the operations.

The Direct Method

In the section of the **Direct Method**, one lists major classes of gross cash receipts and payments and shows cash flows from operating activities. However, this method involves more detailed information on cash flows and so is not used so much in practice; but it gives a better picture of how cash flows through the company.

Steps in Preparing the Direct Method:

1. **Cash Received from Customers:** Report cash received from customers, excluding non-cash revenue.

2. **Cash Paid to Suppliers and Employees:** Subtract cash paid to suppliers and employees, excluding non-cash expenses.

3. **Cash Paid for Operating Expenses:** Include cash outflows related to operating expenses, interest, and taxes.

Example: Consider the following information for ABC Corporation using the direct method:

- Cash received from customers: $495,000

- Cash paid to suppliers and employees: $(485,000)

- Cash paid for interest and taxes: $(25,000)

Journal Entry:

Cash Received from Customers	$ 495,000
Cash Paid to Suppliers and Employees	$ 485,000
Cash Paid for Interest and Taxes	- $ 25,000
Net Cash Flow from Operating Activities	- $ 49,900

Comparison of Methods

The key difference between the **Indirect Method** and the **Direct Method** lies in the approach to presenting cash flows from operating activities:

- The **Indirect Method** reconciles net income with cash flows by adjusting for non-cash transactions and changes in working capital accounts.
- The **Direct Method** lists the actual cash inflows and outflows from operating activities.

Although the **Direct Method** provides more specific understanding of cash movements, the Indirect Method is commonly used due to it applying net income as a beginning balance and simplifying the reconciling the accruals based financial performance against the company's cash based liquidity.

Key Adjustments for Non-Cash Transactions

Regardless of the method used, the following non-cash adjustments are commonly made:

- **Depreciation and Amortization:** Added back to net income since these do not involve actual cash outflows.
- **Gains and Losses on Asset Sales:** Adjusted to remove the impact of non-cash gains or losses, as these do not reflect cash generated or used by operating activities.
- **Changes in Working Capital:** Adjustments for increases and decreases in accounts such as receivables, payables, and inventory to reflect the actual cash movements.

Example of Adjustments:

- **Depreciation Expense**: Added back to net income.
- **Warranty Expense:** Added back to net income.
- **Changes in Accounts Receivable and Accounts Payable:** For accounts where increases or decreases have occurred in the period.

Conclusion

Cash Flow Statement is important to know how a company earns and spends the cash. The Indirect Method and Direct Method give us a good insight of operating cash flows, though the Indirect method is more popular because it reflects in the accrual based financial statements. Through adjustment for the non-cash things and changes in working capital, businesses can get a true picture of the cash graphic and better take care of the liquidity benefit. In the next chapter, we cover investing and financing activities more extensively, to continue the examination of how companies manage the cash flows attributable to long term investments and debt.

CHAPTER 16
FINANCIAL STATEMENTS CONSOLIDATION

Financial Statements consolidation is a relevant process that is implemented when one company (the parent) obtains control over another (the subsidiary). These reflect the parent company's ownership and financial interest in the subsidiary and are used to constitute the group as a single economic entity. Typically, it is the parent company who gains control by holding a majority voting share — often considered more than 50 percent.

Criteria for Consolidation

Consolidated financial statements are required when a parent company gains effective control over an investee, either by:

1. **Majority Ownership:** The voting shares of the subsidiary are in the hands of the parent company. However, if the government imposes constraints on the investee or if the subsidiary is in bankruptcy, control may not be attained in some cases.

2. **Variable Interest Entity (VIE):** The parent is the primary beneficiary of a VIE, even if it does not directly hold voting shares. Control is determined by the ability to direct significant activities of the entity.

3. **Significant Influence:** Alternatively, control may be achievable through a great deal of influence, for example by being able to decide policy matters, or being represented on the board of directors.

Steps for Business Consolidation

When preparing consolidated financial statements, the following steps must be applied:

1. **Identify the Acquirer:** The company that obtains control is the acquirer.

2. **Determine the Acquisition Date:** This is the date the acquirer legally gains control of the subsidiary.

3. **Measure the Fair Value of the Acquired Assets and Liabilities**: All identifiable assets and liabilities must be measured at fair value on the acquisition date, including goodwill or a bargain purchase gain if applicable.

4. **Eliminate Intra Group Balances and Transactions:** Intragroup transactions such as sales, purchases, and loans must be eliminated from the consolidated financial statements.

Goodwill and Bargain Purchases

Goodwill arises when the consideration transferred by the acquirer exceeds the fair value of the identifiable net assets acquired. This amount is recorded as an intangible asset and is not amortized but tested annually for impairment.

Alternatively, if the fair value of the consideration transferred is less than the fair value of the identifiable net assets, the acquirer recognizes a bargain purchase gain in the income statement.

Consolidation at the Date of Acquisition

Upon acquiring a subsidiary, the parent company must adjust the subsidiary's book values to fair value. The acquisition method requires recording the assets and liabilities at their fair value, and any excess consideration over fair value is treated as goodwill.

Example: Suppose Acquirer Corp. acquires 100% of Target Co. by issuing 2,000 shares of stock, valued at $10 each, in exchange for all of Target's net assets. Target's real estate and loan payable are recorded at $50,000 and $20,000, respectively, on the books but have fair values of $72,000 and $22,000. The following adjustments are made to consolidate the financial statements:

Accounts	Acquirer Book Values	Acquiree Book Values	Consolidation Adjustments	Consolidated Balance Sheet
Cash	10,000	4,000		14,000
Real Estate	50,000	16,000	dr. 6,000	72,000
Investment -Acquiree	20,000	0	dr. 15,000	0
Goodwill	0	0	dr. 1,000	1,000
Loan Payable	20,000	5,000	cr. 2,000	27,000
Common Stock	5,000	1,000	cr. 10,000	15,000
Paid in Capital	25,000	12,000	cr. 10,000	35,000
Retained Earnings	10,000	2,000	dr. 2,000	10,000

Intercompany Transactions

When consolidating financial statements, transactions between the parent and subsidiary must be eliminated. This ensures that intragroup transactions, such as sales, purchases, or loans, do not artificially inflate the consolidated financial statements.

Example: Acquirer Corp. purchases 5,000 units of inventory from an unrelated third party at $4/unit. Later, Acquirer sold 5,000 units to Subsidiary Co. at $6/unit. At the year-end, these transactions must be eliminated in the consolidated financial statements as follows:

- Inventory and cost of goods sold (COGS) are adjusted to reflect the pre-transaction balance.

- The journal entries for the consolidation adjustment will reverse any impact on sales, COGS, and inventory that resulted from the intercompany transaction.

This elimination ensures the consolidated statements reflect only transactions with external entities.

Conclusion

Consolidated financial statements are essential for presenting the financial position and results of a parent company and its subsidiaries as a single entity. By eliminating intercompany transactions and adjusting assets and liabilities to fair value, the consolidated statements provide a clearer picture of the economic activities of the corporate group. In this way, stakeholders can assess the collective financial performance, regardless of the number of legal entities involved."

CHAPTER 17
CURRENCY EXCHANGE TRANSACTIONS

The term currency exchange transactions refers to a business that deals with the exchange of one currency for another. These are the kind of transactions that come up when companies buy and sell goods as well as services in foreign markets, borrow and lend funds across national borders and in dealing with foreign subsidiaries. It is important to understand how to account for these transactions properly because changes in currency exchange rates can significantly impact a company's financial results.

GAAP Reporting vs. Tax Reporting

Currency exchange transactions are subject to different treatment under GAAP reporting and tax reporting guidelines:

- **GAAP Reporting:** Unrealized gains or losses from changes in exchange rates between the date of the transaction and the date of payment are recorded in the income statement. These changes affect the value of accounts receivable (AR) and accounts payable (AP) denominated in foreign currency.

- **Tax Reporting:** Taxable income only includes only realized gains or losses. While unrealized gains or losses aren't included in tax computations, they're still reported in GAAP reporting.

GAAP Reporting	Tax Reporting
Record unrealized gain/loss	Exclude from taxable income
Record realized gain/loss	Include in taxable income

Foreign Currency Transactions

A foreign currency transaction is any transaction that results in a receivable or payable that is denominated in a foreign currency. These transactions require special attention because the amount ultimately settled may differ from the amount initially recorded due to changes in the exchange rate.

When these payments are not settled by the end of the reporting period, companies must adjust the value of the outstanding AR or AP to reflect the current exchange rate.

Example: Foreign Currency Sale

Consider a U.S. company (U.S. Co.) that sells goods to a foreign customer for ¥250 on January 1. On the sale date, the spot exchange rate is ¥20 to $1. The company records the AR at the spot rate.

- **Transaction on 1/1:**

- ¥250 / ¥20/$ = $50

Now, assume that by year-end on December 31, the payment has not yet been collected, and the exchange rate has shifted to ¥25 to $1. U.S. Co. must adjust its AR to the new rate:

- **Adjustment on 12/31:**
- ¥250 / ¥25/$ = $35
- Unrealized loss of $15

The company records the following journal entry to adjust the AR and recognize the unrealized loss:

dr. Loss	$	15
cr. Accounts Receivable	$	15

Upon eventual receipt of payment, U.S. Co. records the actual exchange rate gain or loss in its income statement.

Example: Foreign Currency Purchase

Similarly, consider that on October 15, U.S. Co. purchases ¥5,000 worth of goods from a foreign supplier. The spot exchange rate on the purchase date is ¥25 to $1, meaning the AP is initially recorded as $200.

- **Transaction on 10/15:**
- ¥5,000 / ¥25/$ = $200

By year-end, U.S. Co. has not yet made the payment, and the exchange rate has shifted to ¥20 to $1, meaning the AP is now worth $250. The company must record the unrealized loss in its accounts:

dr. Unrealized Loss	$	15
cr. Accounts Payable	$	50

This adjustment reflects the increased cost to settle the AP due to the unfavorable change in the exchange rate.

Accounting for Exchange Rate Changes

Accounting for foreign currency transactions involves recalculating the value of AR and AP based on the current spot exchange rate at each reporting date until the transaction is settled. Changes in the value of these accounts result in either unrealized gains or losses. These gains or losses become realized when the transaction is settled, either through payment or collection.

Key Takeaways

1. **Currency Transaction Accounting:** Both foreign AR and AP are recalculated based on the spot exchange rate at each reporting date.
2. **GAAP vs. Tax Differences:** While unrealized gains and losses are recorded in the financial statements under GAAP, they are excluded from taxable income on tax reporting rules until realized.

3. **Journal Entries:** Exchange rate changes must be properly entered to reduce, but not cancel AR or AP to record gains or losses on the resulting adjusted transactions.

4. **Exchange Rate Calculation**: Make sure you pay attention what direction the rate is changing in. Say that you are converting foreign currency into dollars, so a spot rate should convert correctly for the foreign currency per dollar balance, and then those currency units cancel in the calculation.

Conclusion

In certain situations, when talking foreign currency transactions it is important to grasp how exchange rates are computed and reported. It is for determining correctly what currency is the numerator or denominator of the formula of exchange rate and keeping the agreement throughout all related transactions. Furthermore, foreign exchange rate movements affect cash flow forecasts, hedging strategies and tax planning, increasing both volatility of financial reporting and tax obligations.

This chapter, "Currency Exchange Transactions," brings forth the principles of foreign currency accounting and the way companies adjust their financial statements in the reporting in relation to exchange rates fluctuation. By properly understanding how international trade works, companies can withstand the lurking dangers, but they can still profit from the complexities.

CHAPTER 18
PARTNERSHIP ACCOUNTING

The allocation of income and the changing of partners introduce special difficulties to the partnership accounting. This chapter explores the partnership accounting dynamics of income allocation, restructuring of ownership structure, and dissolution.

Allocation of Partnership Income

Typically, income allocation is defined in a partnership agreement, but if there are no agreements going on, income allocation will follow the general rules depending on how capital is invested, interests, salary, or allocated evenly through profit sharing ratios.

Consider a partnership with two partners, A and B, with a 30:70 profit-sharing agreement. If the partnership earns $8,100 in income for the period, the allocation would proceed as follows:

A Capital	B Capital
$5,000	$6,000
Add Interest on Capital Accounts (10%)	Add Salary to Partner A ($4,000)
$500	$600
$4,000	$0
Allocate Profit Based on Agreement (30:70)	
$900	$2,100
Total After Allocation	
$10,400	$8,700

This table illustrates how each partner's capital account is impacted by the allocation of income, interest, and salary.

Changes in Partnership Structure

Changes in a partnership's ownership structure can occur through the admission of new partners or the retirement of existing partners. Such changes necessitate adjustments to the partnership's equity accounts.

Admission of a New Partner

When a new partner is admitted to a partnership, there are typically two methods for adjusting the capital accounts: the Bonus Method and the Goodwill Method.

1. **Bonus Method:** Any difference between the new partner's contribution and their proportionate share of the partnership's equity is allocated to the existing partners.

Example: Partner A and Partner B have a 40:60 interest in the partnership. The partnership admits Partner C, who contributes $3,000 for a 10% interest. The partnership now has equity of $20,000. The journal entry would be:

Journal Entry - Bonus Method:

dr. Cash	$ 3,000
cr. A Capital	$ 400
cr. B Capital	$ 600
cr. C Capital	$ 2,000

2. **Goodwill Method:** Goodwill is recognized if the new partner's contribution exceeds the existing partnership equity.

Example: Partner A and Partner B admit Partner C. The partnership values C's contribution as generating $30,000 in value. Goodwill is recognized and allocated to the original partners:

Journal Entry - Goodwill Method:

dr. Cash	$ 3,000
dr. Goodwill	$ 10,000
cr. A Capital	$ 4,000
cr. B Capital	$ 6,000
cr. C Capital	$ 3,000

Retirement of a Partner

When a partner retires, the partnership must buy out the partner's interest. Similar to the admission of a new partner, this can be handled using the Bonus Method or the Goodwill Method.

- **Bonus Method:** The capital account of the retiring partner is decreased to match the amount of the payout, and the difference is allocated to the remaining partners.

Journal Entry:

dr. A Capital	$ 1,000
dr. B Capital	$ 2,000
cr. C Capital	$ 5,000

- **Goodwill Method:** Goodwill is recognized and allocated to the remaining partners to reflect the retiring partner's withdrawal from the partnership.

Journal Entry:

dr. Goodwill	$ 10,000
cr. C Capital	$ 5,000
cr. A Capital	$ 4,000
cr. B Capital	$ 6,000

Liquidation of the Partnership

Liquidation occurs when the partnership ceases business operations, and all assets are sold, liabilities are paid, and the remaining assets are distributed to the partners. There are two primary methods for liquidation:

1. **Simple Liquidation (Installment Payments):** Partners are paid as assets are sold off.

2. **Safe Payments Method**: Distribution to partners before all assets are sold, with adjustments for any unsold assets.

Example of Simple Liquidation

Partners A, B, and C have a partnership with a 40:40:20 interest ratio. The balance sheet shows:

Assets	Liabilities	A Capital	B Capital	C Capital
$12,000	$1,000	$3,700	$8,800	-$500

Steps in Liquidation:

1. The partnership sells all assets for $13,000 and pays off liabilities.

2. Distributions are made to the partners based on their capital accounts, ensuring that safe payments are made first..

Journal Entries:

dr. Cash	$ 13,000
dr. Liabilities	$ 1,000
cr. A Capital	$ 100
cr. B Capital	$ 3,700
cr. C Capital	$ 500

3. Final payments are made to the partners according to their capital balances after all assets have been liquidated.

Conclusion

It's no minor undertaking, because partnership accounting is tight on changes on the ownership, how income gets allocated, and the liquidation process. Whether it's relating to the admission

The accounting methods chosen can, or retirement of a partner, or liquidating the entire partnership, have a major impact on how partners equity is calculated and distributed..

CHAPTER 19
GOVERNMENTAL FUND ACCOUNTING

The purpose of this paper is to illustrate governmental fund accounting, which is very crucial in understanding the management and reporting of financials of governments. That is, unlike private sector companies interested in profit and loss, governments are accountable, steward, and transparent. This chapter presents governmental fund accounting by looking at the major principles, fund categories, and practical applications.

Key Sources and Framework of Governmental Accounting

The Governmental Accounting Standards Board sets out a certain guideline for government accounting. The hierarchy of authoritative GAAP for governmental entities is as follows:

1. Category A: GASB Statements and Interpretations.

2. Category B: GASB Technical Bulletins and Implementation Guides.

Governmental financial reporting serves a core purpose of accountability to the public. But it gives the public the ability to review how much the government spends and raises and spends it to fulfill their commitment.

GAAP Hierarchy and Fund Structure

The **hierarchy of authoritative GAAP** sources are governmental accounting standards board (GASB) Statements and Interpretations. Governmental accounting is structured around a number of funds and the structure for each is a self-balancing set of accounts established for differing purposes. These funds can be classified into three categories: governmental funds, proprietary funds, and fiduciary funds.

1. Governmental Funds: They include general fund, special revenue funds, capital projects funds, debt service funds and permanent funds. The modified accrual basis of accounting is used by governmental funds where revenues are accrued when measurable and available, and when expenditures are accrued when incurred, accounted for in the related liability. The accounting equation for these funds is:

Current Assets + Deferred Outflows of Resources - Current Liabilities - Deferred Inflows of Resources = Fund Balance.

2. Proprietary Funds: These funds include enterprise funds and internal service funds and use the **full accrual basis of accounting**, similar to for-profit entities. The accounting equation for proprietary funds is:

Assets + Deferred Outflows of Resources - Liabilities - Deferred Inflows of Resources = Net Position.

4. **Fiduciary Funds:** These include custodial funds, investment trust funds, pension trust funds, and private-purpose trust funds. Like proprietary funds, they follow the full accrual basis of accounting and use the same accounting equation as proprietary funds.

Government-Wide Financial Statements

Governmental entities prepare **government-wide financial statements** that consolidate governmental and proprietary funds but exclude fiduciary funds. These statements include the **statement of net position** and the **statement of activities.** Net position in these statements is categorized into three components:

- **Net investment in capital assets**: Represents capital assets, net of accumulated depreciation and related debt.
- **Restricted net position:** Reflects constraints imposed by external parties or laws.
- **Unrestricted net position:** Represents the residual balance of net position after subtracting net investment in capital assets and restricted amounts.

The Concept of Fund Balance

Within governmental funds, the fund balance serves as the equity component. It is classified into five categories:

- **Nonspendable:** Includes amounts not in spendable form (e.g., inventories) or legally or contractually required to remain intact.
- **Restricted:** Amounts constrained for specific purposes by external parties or legislation.
- **Committed**: Funds earmarked for specific purposes by formal government action.
- **Assigned:** Amounts intended for specific purposes but not committed by formal government action.
- **Unassigned:** Represents the residual classification for the general fund.

Modified Accrual Basis of Accounting

Governmental funds use the **modified accrual basis** of accounting, which differs from the accrual basis used in proprietary and fiduciary funds. Revenues are recognized when both measurable and available, and expenditures are recognized when incurred. However, **long-term assets and liabilities** are not recognized on the balance sheet; they are recorded off-balance sheet until their settlement impacts financial resources.

Example: Property tax revenues are recognized when the taxes are assessed and expected to be collected within the current period, typically defined as within 60 days after year-end. Conversely, expenditures for capital assets, debt repayment, and supplies are recognized when the related liabilities are incurred.

Government-Wide Financial Statements

Government-wide financial statements provide a comprehensive overview of the government's financial position and activities. These statements consolidate all of the government's funds except for fiduciary funds and provide a long-term focus on the government's finances:

- **Statement of Net Position:** This balance sheet-like statement presents the government's assets, liabilities, and net position.
- **Statement of Activities:** This income statement-like report details the government's revenues, expenses, and changes in net position.

Modified Accrual Accounting

The modified accrual basis of accounting is unique to governmental funds. It focuses on current financial resources and does not account for long-term assets and liabilities. Revenue recognition occurs when it is both measurable and available, usually within 60 days of the fiscal year-end. Expenditures are recognized when the related liability is incurred, except for interest on long-term debt, which is recognized when due.

Budgetary Accounting

Governmental entities employ budgetary accounting to ensure that expenditures do not exceed authorized amounts. Encumbrances represent commitments related to unperformed contracts for goods and services, which help prevent overspending. When a government places an order, it records an encumbrance, reducing the amount of uncommitted budgetary resources. As expenditures occur, the encumbrances are reversed, and the actual expenditure is recorded.

Comprehensive Annual Financial Report (CAFR)

Many governmental entities prepare a Comprehensive Annual Financial Report (CAFR), which provides a more detailed view of financial performance than standard financial reports.

A CAFR typically consists of:

- **Introductory Section:** Contains a transmittal letter, organizational chart, and other general information.

- **Financial Section:** Includes the independent auditor, a report, government-wide financial statements, and fund financial statements, along with required supplementary information (RSI).

- **Statistical Section:** Provides financial trends, demographic information, and other data to offer additional context for financial performance.

Governmental Fund Transactions

Governmental fund accounting involves a variety of transactions. Some common examples include:

1. Tax Revenues: Property taxes and sales taxes represent major revenue sources for governmental funds. Revenues are recognized when they become measurable and available to finance expenditures of the current fiscal year.

2. Transfers Between Funds: Governments often transfer resources from one fund to another for specific purposes. These transfers are recorded as other financing sources in the receiving fund and other financing uses in the transferring fund.

3. Debt Service and Capital Projects: Governmental funds track expenditures related to repaying

Encumbrance Accounting: Governments often use encumbrance accounting to reserve part of the budget for future expenditures. Encumbrances are commitments related to unperformed contracts or purchase orders. Encumbrances are recorded when the government places an order for goods or services, reducing the available fund balance.

General Fund Accounting

The General Fund is the primary operating fund for most governments and accounts for all financial resources not accounted for in other funds. Key transactions include budgeting, tax revenue collection, and expenditure for general governmental services like public safety and education.

Example Journal Entries for the General Fund:

1. Budget Adoption: The government adopts a budget at the beginning of the fiscal year, recording estimated revenues and appropriations.

dr. Estimated Revenues	$ 50,000
cr. Appropriations	$ 40,000
cr. Budgetary Fund Balance	$ 10,000

2. Tax Collection: Governments record property tax revenues and recognize receivables even if not all the taxes are collected immediately.

dr. Property Taxes Receivable	$ 40,000
dr. Estimated Uncollectible Taxes	$ 4,000
cr. Revenues	$ 36,000

3. Expenditures: Expenditures are recognized when incurred, such as salaries or utilities.

dr. Expenditures	$ 35,000
dr. Vouchers Payable	$ 35,000

4. Encumbrances: When a government issues a purchase order, it records an encumbrance to reserve budget authority.

dr. Encumbrances	$ 500
cr. Budgetary Fund Balance - Committed	$ 4,000

Proprietary and Fiduciary Fund Accounting

Proprietary Funds: These funds account for government activities that operate similarly to private-sector businesses. The full accrual basis of accounting is used, and proprietary funds are expected to be self-sustaining through user charges. For example, a government-run water utility would be accounted for using a proprietary fund.

Fiduciary Funds: These funds account for resources the government holds on behalf of others, such as pension trust funds or investment trust funds. Fiduciary funds are excluded from government-wide financial statements because the government does not have control over these resources.

Conclusion:

Governmental accounting emphasizes accountability and stewardship of public resources. By adhering to the modified accrual basis for governmental funds and the full accrual basis for proprietary and fiduciary funds, governments ensure that their financial reporting meets the needs of the public and other stakeholders. Accurate and transparent financial reporting is critical for maintaining public trust and ensuring that governments fulfill their obligations efficiently and effectively.

CHAPTER 20
NON- PROFIT FINANCIAL MANAGEMENT

Financial management by not-for-profit organizations is different in terms of such accounting practices and principles. This transparency and accountability guides non profits, with a focus to ensure funds are actually used to further their mission. Not for profit organizations financial statements consist of Statement of Financial Position, Statement of Activities, Statement of Cash Flow and the related notes.

Statement of Financial Position

This is the balance sheet for non-profit organizations. It includes assets, liabilities, and net assets. The key difference from for-profit entities is the classification of net assets:

1. **Net Assets without Donor Restrictions:** These assets have no donor-imposed restrictions. Donations are unrestricted if the governing board has the ability to use them at its discretion in the current year.

2. **Net Assets with Donor Restrictions:** These assets are restricted either temporarily or permanently by the donor. The restrictions could be related to time or specific purposes and may involve mandates that prevent the use of principal indefinitely.

Example Statement of Financial Position:
XYZ Foundation
Statement of Financial Position
For the Year Ended December 31, 20X4

	Amount
Assets	
Cash	$XX,XXX
Receivables	$XX,XXX
Total Assets	$XX,XXX
Liabilities	
Accounts Payable	$XX,XXX
Loans Payable	$XX,XXX
Total Liabilities	$XX,XXX
Net Assets	
Without Donor Restrictions	$XX,XXX
With Donor Restrictions	$XX,XXX
Total Net Assets	$XX,XXX

Statement of Activities

The Statement of Activities is equivalent to the income statement in for-profit entities. It shows changes in net assets during the year, broken down between activities with and without donor restrictions.

Example Statement of Activities:

XYZ Foundation
Statement of Activities
For the Year Ended December 31, 20X4

	Amount
Changes in Net Assets Without Donor Restrictions	
Contribution Revenues	$XX,XXX
Investment Gains	$X,XXX
Expenses	($XX,XXX)
Net Change	$X,XXX
Changes in Net Assets With Donor Restrictions	
Contribution Revenues	$X,XXX
Investment Income	$X,XXX
Net Assets Released from Restrictions	$X,XXX
Change in Total Net Assets	$XX,XXX
Beginning Net Assets	$XX,XXX
Ending Net Assets	$XX,XXX

Revenues

Non-profit organizations recognize two types of revenues:

1. **Contribution Revenue:** This is money received with nothing expected in return. Contributions can come with or without donor restrictions and are recognized either when received or when donor conditions are met.

2. **Exchange Revenue:** This is revenue earned by providing goods or services, such as program fees or membership dues. Exchange revenue must come without donor restrictions.

Endowments and Net Assets Released from Restrictions

Endowments consist of donations where the principal remains intact either indefinitely (permanent endowment) or for a specific time period (term endowment). When restrictions are met or the time period expires, net assets are released from restriction and moved into the "without donor restrictions" category.

Example of Net Assets Released from Restriction:

1. Upon receiving a $750 contribution with restrictions:

dr. Cash	$	750
cr. Contribution Revenue- Donor - Restricted	$	750

2. When the restriction is met and the funds are spent:

dr. Program Expense	$	750
cr. Cash	$	750
cr. Contribution Revenue Without Donor Restriction	$	750

Statement of Cash Flows

Non-profit organizations must report their cash flows similarly to for-profit entities. Cash flows from operating activities include contributions and exchange revenue, while cash flows from investing and financing activities include endowment transactions and long-term restrictions.

Other Important Items and Transactions

- **Endowments:** Permanent and term endowments dictate how funds can be used based on donor-imposed restrictions.

- **Pledges:** Pledges are recognized as receivables, and revenue is only recorded when the donation is unconditional and the likelihood of collection is high.

- **Donated Services**: If a specialized service is donated, such as professional labor, it is recognized at fair value as both a revenue and an expense.

- **Agent Transactions:** If a not-for-profit serves as an agent collecting funds for other organizations, it records the transaction as a liability rather than revenue.

Gains and Losses on Investment

Investments DO include unrealized gains or losses as measured by non profit organizations. All types of securities, including debt are included and investments are measured at fair value.

Conditional Contributions

Contributions by conditions are not considered revenue until the donor's conditions are substantially met. The difference between a condition and a restriction is key: Money can be used only according to a restriction, but not at all under a condition of whether money can be considered revenue.

Deferred Revenue

Deferred revenue is also recognized by non profit organizations who receive and collect money in advance of providing services in the future.

The first part of this chapter details the key elements of non profit accounting, arguments over donor access ability to restricted monies, endowment management, and the necessity for financial reporting that is sensible for transparency and accountability.

Conclusion

Management of financials for a non-profit is a sensitive issue and requires prudent attention to donor restrictions, endowment treatment, and transparency in financial reporting. Unlike for profit entities, nonprofits must run distinct types of funds: unrestricted and restricted, and funds have to be properly classified and spent in keeping with donor intent. The pledge, endowment, and donated services recognition makes the financial landscape further complicated and precise record keeping and GAAP standards for nonprofits are required. Financial management and reporting are effective because they are not only a means of being compliant to legal requirements and regulatory requirements but they also build trust with donors, stakeholders, and the general public. Having prepared and published accurate and transparent financial statements, non profit organizations are able to show their dedication to their cause and appropriate use of the resources they have been given.

FINAL CONCLUSION

From the essential principles and practices needed to make sense of and effectively control financial information to the measurable business impact of accounting, this book has shown you a comprehensive journey through the world of modern accounting. The book presents the content from the foundations of monetary assets and liabilities through to the detailed aspects of governmental and nonprofit accounting, aimed at exposing readers to a solid framework of accounting knowledge.

Using current monetary assets and liabilities as a foundation, we proceeded through the neediness of handling lease accounting, debt restructuring, and investment accounting. Each chapter builds upon the other to form a unified story of accounting's role within business decision making, financial management, and regulatory compliance. We grew our understanding of how accounting works in different contexts (from partnership dynamics to non-profit financial management) as we entered into more advanced topics like governmental fund accounting.

This book is all about the notion that accounting is more than just using numbers in spreadsheets; it is the cornerstone of financial decision making. Proper accounting ensures transparency, trust, and efficient use of resources for businesses, governments, and nonprofits. Chapters introduced concepts of accruals, taxation, investments, and consolidation as tools that any professional who wishes to manage finances properly in today's complex economic environment.

We need to conclude with the fact that accounting comes with a change in time. Whether brought on by new regulatory changes, technological advancements, business practice changes, or what have you, the accounting landscape is everchanging to keep up with the needs of a world in flux. By understanding the principles discussed in this book, readers will be able to grow more confident in taking these changes in stride and more skillfully apply accounting concepts to their professional lives.

What I have learned here is not just a foundation, but a launch pad for further accounting exploration and application to other real world contexts. It's with this solid footing that anyone reading will continue to grow professionally, feel a sense of successful worth, and come to appreciate the vital function accounting plays within any and all industries.

Made in United States
Orlando, FL
01 March 2025